Gurkha Highlander

Gurkha Highlander

WALKING MALLAIG TO STONEHAVEN

Neil Griffiths

Cualann Press

ISBN 0 9544416 3 X

First Edition 2004

British Library Cataloguing in Publication Data. A catalogue record of
this book is available at the British Library.

Printed by Bell & Bain, Glasgow

Published by Cualann Press Limited, 6 Corpach Drive, Dunfermline,
KY12 7XG Scotland
Tel/Fax 01383 733724
Email: cualann@btinternet.com
Website: www.cualann-scottish-books.co.uk

Dedication

I wish to dedicate *Gurkha Highlander* to my parents, Ann and Duncan, who are responsible for all my good points. The bad ones are entirely my own.

The Route: Mallaig to Stonehaven

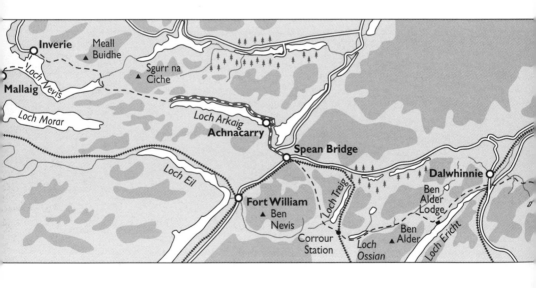

<< The Atlantic Ocean

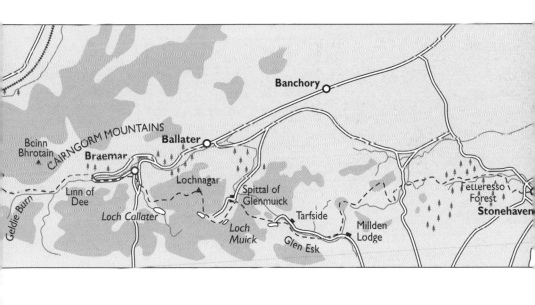

The North Sea >>

Contents

Introduction

When Sergeant Dhal Bahadur Dhal asked at the end of our 340 kilometre Southern Upland Way march: 'So, Neil Saheb, what are we doing next year?' I merely laughed. Then in the following spring, almost unthinkingly, I began checking out Gurkha availability, booking a vehicle, accommodation and newspaper adverts. Before it really sank in, there was a massive and foolhardy walk marked in my diary for the end of July.

The concept of marching off road from Mallaig on the Atlantic coast to Stonehaven on the North Sea, over the roof of Scotland with men from the roof of the world, was attractive on paper. Well, of course it was. We'd see some of the country's finest scenery, have the time of our lives and raise money for the surviving 12,000 wartime Gurkhas now living in penury in the high Himalayas.

There was one technical, nay physiological problem. Just how tough was the walking? And could I not only keep up but enjoy myself alongside some of the hardiest, fittest soldiers in the world?

Frankly, my dears, it was a bit of a struggle but the legendary stamina and high spirits of my merry men both shamed and pulled me through. They are, indeed, everything you've ever read about, and that we were helping their glorious forebears made them all blaze with a pride that gave the trek its driving, inescapable force. I had to keep up.

We weren't alone. The Royal British Legion Scotland rallied wholeheartedly to the call and raised £10,000 without ever wishing thanks. This was a duty, a debt of honour, but for me, and my Gurkha colleagues, each cheque was a joyous vindication and cause for heartfelt gratitude. Similarly, enormous thanks go to the thousands of 'ordinary' Scots who couldn't stop themselves posting a donation and thereby creating the type of mini avalanche of mail that causes such crises these days to our otherwise totally reliable Post Office.

Members of Her Majesty's Press aided the cause with happy enthusiasm too, especially Jim Crumley, Simon Pia, Susan Mansfield, Fordyce Maxwell, Albert Morris, Rab McNeil, Tom Morton and Mike Wade. Of course, they unfailingly scrutinised every fact and quote, though we still joke about Alan Mackay's BBC Scotland TV report in which he twice, accidentally, assured viewers that he had walked with us.

It's difficult to know how exactly the history of the Second World War would read without 250,000 Gurkhas coming to our aid, men who fought everywhere from El Alamein to Burma, but it's certain that things would be different. Without a quarter of a million of the best soldiers in the world, events could not have been the same. What is clear though is that those men, from a country that is not even in the Commonwealth, deserve a small stipend by way of thanks. Most did not serve the requisite fifteen years for a pension but they were bonny fechters who deserve something. The GWT pays them, and 5,000 widows, a £5 per week pension. Admittedly, this is not much, even in Nepal, but it is the difference between total destitution and survival. Plus, it is important to these old men and women to know that Britain has not forgotten them. Most of us haven't, as I hope this book proves. There have been three Gurkha Highlander Mallaig to Stonehaven marches, and this is the tale of our first, in 2001. Each has raised an average of £70,000; so clearly, Britain remembers the Gurkhas.

The whole blasted trek would not have been possible without the help of some special people. Joanna Lumley may be a celebrated actress to some, but in Nepalese circles she's the daughter of a famous Gurkha officer, Major Jimmy Lumley, and a well kent benefactor of the Trust. Her stupendous generosity provided the seed capital for the entire venture, and in addition, her early words of encouragement were pivotal to our proceeding or staying at home. Thanks, Joanna.

Then there's the extraordinary Leigh Howieson who had the necessary pragmatism to transform some of my flights of fancy into the mundane: adverts, press releases and mail shots. Alas, this bit is merely an intro, not a stand-alone book, but Leigh's work deserves more. Her motto? Never wrong, never vague. Thanks, Leigh.

And John Hobkirk, our accountant, the practice manager of Taits WS of Kelso, who just about broke his back on a daily basis to ensure that the financial side was kept in strict soldier-like order. There was never a '1' when there should have been a '2', and that, my friends, is damn clever. Especially when you are doing it for zero pounds. I send you, John, 10x10 thanks (receipt in the post).

My brother Ewen gets a fair bit of stick in this tale but that's just my jolly fraternal way. Ewen's down-to-earth analysis was always, er, welcome, and there's no doubt in my mind that his heart is at least as big as his enormous feet. Ewen is responsible for this cover as well as that of *Gurkha Reiver* (available via www.cualann-scottish-books.co.uk). Thanks, Bro'.

I'm tempted to thank Gyan Dhal, Dil, Surendra and Chandra, but they all had a brilliant holiday which they appreciated very much and need no special words of thanks. Just joking, Thanks, boys. You'll go far. In fact, 200 miles that-a-way.

Two tips for would-be authors. Firstly, don't, for God's sake, ever criticise anyone in print you don't know very well, no matter how jocular – or deserved. The repercussions far outweigh your forgotten wee joke. Secondly, your mum, wife or partner will wonder why you haven't dedicated your book to their immortal memory. So dedicate your book to somebody. Just small points that become big ones. I know. I was that soldier.

And to you who have bought this book, thanks a million. I beg you not to lend it to anyone. Insist they buy their own. Be rude.

To those of you who wish to imitate me, please do. This is a great cause and needs your help. Life is one big adventure, so grab it with both hands. Presuming you have two; this is not bi-handedism – all Gurkha books strive to include socially those with one hand or less.

You never know what will happen. Circumstances will never quite explain how Julian Clarey ended up promoting *Gurkha Reiver* in Edinburgh in the 2003 Festival, but he did.

Bless the Gurkhas and bless the Scots! Jai Gurkhali ra jai Scotisharu!

Neil Griffiths

Overleaf. **Friends in high places.**

I

Knoydart

~~~

I 've always found it vaguely surprising that clouds are silent. There they are, filling up the sky, large or small, moving quickly, drifting or just mooching about. In flimsy wisps, or huge, rising galleons, brilliant white, or pink and trimmed with gold, bruised blue or Scottish grey, they are always with us. Part of our everyday life, but unlike almost everything else in nature that moves, they're without a soundtrack. Admittedly, there's the occasional thunderstorm but, sorry, they don't count because it's actually electricity that's making all that noise, not the cloud itself.

To be walking in the thick of one, up a long Knoydart mountain track, was to be damp, blind and near deaf. The low-lying cloud hid the dreamy scenery of Loch Nevis, the Sound of Sleat and the Isle of Skye. We were missing unmissable world-class views, but worst of all, the mist hid the blasted route itself. We were unable to gauge progress, nor see how far away was the top of the pass which marked the end of the climb. It was like tramping up a sodden treadmill with no way of knowing when it would all end. Terrific.

There were several other factors working agin me. Ahead scampered my colleagues, five serving Gurkhas, who were travelling thoughtlessly, selfishly, far too fast. Coming from the high Himalayas, today was a mere saunter in the hills for them. But not for me; my forty-four year old lungs were going like industrial bellows, and my vision was beginning to swim, as I mindlessly, proudly, attempted to keep up.

'You okay, Bro'?' called my brother Ewen from above. What a morale-booster. He didn't seem to be even puffing.

'Shall I answer and waste precious breath?' I wondered, trying not to stumble as rain pattered down, and torrents sluiced between my boots as if the sky were being emptied further uphill. In a brainless show of braggadocio, I kept going but when I caught up, the guys cheerfully strode away into the mist. This was too much.

My heart was rocking on its mountings. Can people die of a heart attack at forty-four? My mind flew to Richard Beckinsale. Yes, they can. My thighs were not just screaming but were in the grip of a fiery vice. Thighs can't actually explode, can they?

Embarrassing pop tunes from my youth began to play in my head. *Chirpy, Chirpy, Cheep, Cheep.* I could even remember the opening lines and recall the group's name, Middle of the Road. Which little alleys in my mind had been unlocked?

'I'm hallucinating,' I thought. 'Any minute now the music will be booming out across the glen and I'll know I've gone, completely gone.'

The five-kilometre rise had started gradually but as the slope increased, so, it seemed, did the speed of the boys. Somewhere to our right could be heard the sounds of an engorged stream, its water crashing and careering down to the sea loch of Loch Nevis. Now, comfortingly, its noise was diminishing. Sweat poured off me, my temples dripping and boots slipping.

Like an old man in a bad poem, I eventually came across the group, squatting near the head of the pass, wolfing down sandwiches, their packs lying like upturned turtles. Big white grins lit up the gloom.

'Are we at the top?'

'Think so, we've only got a small climb and we're there,' answered Gyan.

The cold and damp, unnoticed until we stopped, laid clammy fingers on us, prodding us on our way before muscles seized up. On another July day, one with sun and blue skies, we'd have been rooted to the spot by the sheer exhilaration of what lay below us: the glen down to Inverie, the Isle of Eigg set in sapphire to the west, the long mouth of Loch Nevis with the whole view held in the rocky arms of Beinn Bhuidhe and Meall Buidhe on whose pass we now stood. But today the Almighty had brought the shutters down and literally left us in the cold.

Earlier this morning the team had disembarked on to the Mallaig quayside and taken in the low-lying cloud without comment. The town has been described as being created solely to supply Glasgow with kippers, that it sits snarling at you like a junkyard dog but, frankly, it seemed too tepid a place to incite passionate comment. It was no more remarkable than a dozen Highland ports, and being a place of transit was implicitly a place of come and go.

Pre-expedition excitement meant the boys only wanted to get out and hit the twenty-mile walk across Knoydart as quickly as possible and to hell with the elements. It is this attitude that makes them such excellent soldiers; they never moan, and have a driving energy that sees every enemy cast aside and smashed to pieces.

'Parade! Parade, smile!' ordered Chandra, holding a little camera. We formed up with fishing boats, a dull sea and grey sky as a backdrop with loud arguments as to who should take the picture. 'I go first!' 'No, I go first!' Modern bungalows dotted the immediate locality but our eyes were on the weather. Driving up the Morar peninsula minutes before (The Road to the Isles, Rathad nan Eilean), the sky had darkened to the point where headlights were essential. We were horrified to spot road-workers in midge head nets. I had not anticipated the threat of Scotland's smallest team player but locals always know conditions best and the promise of a bad day loomed as a dead cert.

Entering a small, unlit shed with the hopeful 'Ticket Office' above the door, it was possible to discern a Highlander sitting behind a tiny square table, his long legs straight out and protruding on to 'my' side.

'Yes?' he asked brightly, almost cheekily, as if welcoming me to Heathrow.

I grinned too. 'This where I can get seven tickets for Bruce Watt's ferry to Inverie?'

The guy peeled off seven little tickets like an old-fashioned bus conductor, if you can envisage one in check-shirt and a two-day old beard. And, yes, a receipt was beyond him, but perhaps the ferry's owner could provide all the high tech stuff.

In fact the ferry, *The Western Isles*, was cool, taking about half an hour to cross Loch Nevis to the little community of Inverie, arriving just before 11 a.m. The dark sea was flat as glass and guillemots popped and dived around us. The south coast looked horribly wild, with steep sides and stunted bush. To the east, in Wagnerian gloom, stood the mountains we'd have to negotiate, but today, capped in heavy cloud, only the lower reaches were visible. The light played on this immense scene as if part Tolkein and part *Twilight of the Gods*. A slim shaft of sun struck a war memorial at the head of the glen as if this were theatre and not real life.

Gyan's sudden question brought me back to reality: 'I hope you know how to use those?'

I had been fingering a GPS as we stood together, leaning over the shiprail, and was frankly irritated to be on the receiving end of such sharp suspicion. 'Er, yes, Gyan. This year we're so far from civilisation I thought it would be a good idea to know exactly where we were.'

'Just testing,' he replied unconvinced. An instructor and staff sergeant at the Royal School of Signals in Dorset, Gyan was obviously still in role.

I exchanged looks with my brother, who rolled his eyes. Just you watch it, Gyan. Instead of ensuring our junior colleagues had all the right kit, Gyan was checking on *me*. We were spread out in the open bow, sitting on luggage, coils of rope and wherever we could find a seat, chatting to the twenty or so fellow passengers. Our trek had received good pre-march publicity and 'I've read about you in the papers' was a frequent opener, though Scots and Gurkhas inevitably want to talk and no premise was necessary. Two of our men didn't speak much English but the smiles and nods said more than words anyway. That folk seemed impressed with our trek re-introduced both a sense of pride and foreboding.

'You're walking to Stonehaven, that's miles!' exclaimed one backpacker with extraordinary perception – perhaps he had a GPS. Yes, two-hundred miles off road to the North Sea in eight days is pretty far, but our route paid homage to the old-fashioned idea of the high pass. Highlanders of yore didn't climb mountain peaks at all, they had no need to, and when they moved across the land it was to travel and not to experience happy hiking high jinks. In the short, uncertain and uncomfortable life spans of the time, folk did not seek extra toil; climbing mountains was profitless and unnecessary. They were dangerous and barren places without attraction. Our Gurkhas, too, knew this from the cradle. The quickest way to reach the North Sea from here would be to go between any silly obstacles like summits and that's what we were doing. I had come across the route in an old guidebook. Its official name, *The Twelve Passes*, had a fine publicity-friendly ring to it.

The boat was soon berthed at Inverie. It felt like we'd arrived at an island but the Knoydart peninsula is, fortunately for us, part of the mainland. Try asking your computer for a road route from Mallaig to Inverie, stand well back and watch it have a wee tantrum as it realises that they should be connected but aren't. We were last off. *'Ayo Gurkhali!'* (The Gurkahs are coming!) I shouted and the whole team howled it as one – it is their war cry – and charged over the gangplank, laughing. Surendra was helping a BT engineer carry a metal trunk ashore. He looked at me and loudly announced: 'In twenty-five years, this is the first time anyone has ever helped me with my gear!' For a moment I wondered why he hadn't simply mentioned this to Surendra (there is a British belief that these foreign chappies don't understand unless spoken to at volume 10) but I quickly understood: he wasn't just expressing appreciation; he was also reproaching the whole community.

Gyan and Dhal, a staff sergeant and a sergeant in the Queen's Gurkha Signals, had been with me the year before on another walk, and were all you could want from experienced NCOs. Completely steady, good-humoured and tarmac tough. Built from the Gurkha handbook, they shared the same low-rise brick-built physique of the true hillboy, with thick-set legs designed for scaling the biggest mountains on the planet.

We had been joined by three from the 2nd Battalion The Royal Gurkha Rifles, based at Folkestone: Dil, Surendra and Chandra. The RGR boys were on local leave and their British officer had been delighted, if not astonished, to be able to put them in my hands for a seven-day hike.

'You mean you're gonna feed, clothe and house them? Well, that's great! We try to give them something to do on their local leaves, otherwise they hang around the barracks or are down various pubs spending their cash, and meeting suspicious characters.'

Of course, I was not a dodgy person and they'd rarely see a pint of lager, would they? The man who made up the magnificent seven was my younger brother, Ewen, a thirty-three year old graphic designer who seemed terrifyingly fit. He actually visited health clubs *and* used their exercise machines. As to who exactly re-set the milometres so that their runners would have to jog for two miles before the dial showed one, is a subject upon which my lips remain sealed.

Overleaf. *Left:* **Mallaig. Do you guys know what you're doing? Our vessel is on the right.**
Right: **Guerrillas in the mist? Near the top of our first pass.**
Next two pages: *Left:* **Last sight of the Atlantic – the east end of Loch Nevis (the picture I sent to Sir Cameron Mackintosh).**
Right: **Knoydart snack break before hammering through to Glen Dessarry.**

The walk began in shafting rain with a surprisingly difficult map-reading puzzle to find the right track to exit the tiny village. The rain splashed the rhododendrons and thick moss atop the stane dykes as we followed the track up towards Gleann an Dubh-Lochan. Gyan had decided, in a moment of pomposity when we bought the shorts, socks and boots in Edinburgh, that he alone had to have long trousers that could cleverly unzip into shorts should the occasion arise. Ewen and I groaned, but here he was today removing the muddy lower halves of the blasted things. He was never to wear them again.

Ewen and I grinned at each other.

Having crossed a bridge (and our first contour at ten metres) over the River Inverie and tramped through a birch wood, we had our first break at five miles beside a locked bothy. The area is one of Europe's wettest and nature showed no signs of letting up today. Knoydart acts as the bows of mainland Britain, taking everything that the North Atlantic blows in, its craggy peaks and acid bogs shaped and created over aeons of elemental battering. We were in its very bowsprit. Not surprisingly, it's a very lonely place.

'This is like home!' smiled the cheery Chandra, a Limbu from east Nepal, looking up at the barren cloud-clad landscape. The hills were a damp green dotted with car-size rocks. His features were near Tibetan, whose language was still spoken by his grandparents. Surendra had surreptitiously slapped a Gurkha Welfare Trust sticker on the back of his colleague's head, explaining: 'He look Chinee' and that label now clarified matters. In fact, to me, Chandra could have been Japanese. Like most Limbus, Chandra was slight of build, light-skinned and mischievous. But he was a Gurkha and, like his clansman, Kali, from the year before, his build gave little hint as to the sheer strength that lay within him. 'My name means Moon!' he'd beamed but his bright smile was sunny.

Surendra was a Tamang, like Gyan, and from east Nepal too. Tall and slim, he didn't look like your usual Gurkha but he'd just passed the airborne forces' selection course and was clearly a capable, conscientious young man. Just back from Sierra Leone was Dilkamur, Prince of Hearts, a handsome, broad-set Rai with bulging calves and ready grin. A corporal and very bright, his English was excellent and he had a near supernatural ability to see a map in 3D. Such were the men that I caught up with in the motionless greyness of our first pass. 'Faith, there was little small about them save the question of their size.'

At the time I was unaware of Dil's skills with a map. Map-reading in mist – would you believe it – is difficult but at the turn for this glen I had been totally certain that we were on the correct route. We conferred, of course; to have taken men up the wrong glen would have been catastrophic to my pride and the team's morale. We were too remote today, too out-of-the-way, to start making mistakes. There are no roads in Knoydart, our pick-up vehicle awaited over at Loch Arkaig; only our boots could get us there. Plus, if I couldn't walk these hills without pain, I at least wanted to be able to map-read them comfortably. To be unable to do both would be too embarrassing.

Gyan was right. We were two minutes from the top and for a moment there was a glimpse of Loch Nevis far below as we crested the pass and the clouds briefly parted.

'Neil Saheb!' called Dhal, thumping down the muddy track to the loch. 'Next time, is it possible we walk along the edge of the loch instead of this climb?' Dhal, like a true piper, had to be difficult and was even wearing blue shorts instead of the uniform light brown.

'It may not seem like it, but we've taken a short cut. The route along the loch is practically impassable, anyway. Check out the map. Big cliffs, crags and rough stuff all the way.' I'd read earlier about how Bishop James Gordon had scrambled along the shoreline, sometimes on all fours in 1707, complaining that he was 'beset with precipices and morasses'. It wouldn't have changed in three hundred years.

'No, Dhal! Can't be done … ARGH!' I howled as I fell on my bum. The whole of Knoydart seemed to be made of only rock, mud and mat grass. Too wild even for heather, the Rough Bounds is a tough place. Even so, I knew why Dhal had asked. Why go from Loch Nevis, over a huge mountain to then descend to the same sea loch and start again? Seems unlikely, but it is the easiest route.

'We'd never make it without a path along the shore!' I yelled back, slipping savagely like an Italian in the six-yard box. 'How come no-one else falls over like me?'

'Because you're holding the map!' laughed Ewen. 'Plus you're a complete prat!'

The steep descent took only minutes, and then we were in a new world where the air stood still and the sun burned warmly. It was totally silent too, and a sense of remoteness took us by surprise. We were alone together. The black roofless ruins of three small buildings reminded us that man had once struggled, and failed, to live here. The overgrown site stood as a metaphor and recalled the words of Donald Ross, a journalist in the 1850s, who, describing the peninsula's clearances, wrote: 'the voice of man is gone from Knoydart.'

'It looks okay,' guessed Gyan, as we inspected a wobbly footbridge which spanned a shallow, rushing river. A series of planks held in place by wire, hanging from two hawsers, it certainly looked no safer than 'okay' but was definitely on the wrong side of 'totally secure'. 'Surendra will go first,' ordered Gyan with a magnificent attempt at total confidence.

Our boy laughed as he grabbed the suspension bridge's two steel ropes, the slats swinging left and right with each step. Flimsy, yes, but not ready to collapse into the stream today. It was probably more robust than most in the Himalayas. We were all over in seconds, hooting as the thing swung to and fro. We went one at a time though.

Towering mountains surrounded us on three sides, their summits linked by cloud, while Loch Nevis hemmed us in on the fourth. The far shore and tousled backdrop, unlike most British coastlines, were without roads. We were far from anything.

'This is great!' announced Dhal, matter of fact. Nobody had said anything but we sat down for a coffee as one and took in the stillness of this silent spot.

Looking back at the ruins, the ever-curious Dil asked: 'Did people live here once?'

'Oh, God, yes,' I groaned, pushing fingers melodramatically through my hair. 'Difficult to believe but there were a lot of folk here once.'

The Knoydart settlements of Skiary, Runival, Barrisdale, Inverdorchail, Inverguseran, Airor, Doune, Sandaig and even Inverie were all destroyed over a violent few days in April 1853 when factor James Grant and his henchmen pushed over walls, slaughtered livestock and herded the terrified cottars aboard the merchantman *Sillary* for paid transport to Australia. The Macdonnells of Glengarry had run up huge debts and were selling their land to an English forgemaster who wanted only an estate for the then fashionable black-faced sheep. Sixteen refused to go and, like vermin, took to the hills. Their clansmen, on the whim of the *Sillary*'s captain, were taken, not to New South Wales, but Nova Scotia.

The imported sheep proved financially ruinous (I'd guess we're talking far less than one ewe per hectare) and the estate was quickly turned over to deer stalking.

As late as 1948 there was the Knoydart Landgrab in which a handful of Highlanders staked a claim to the crofts of their forebears under the misapprehension that the new Labour government would ignore the rule of law. Men toiled on the land, tilling the thin soil with all the fear and hope of the desperate. But Ceres looked away and London's guineas weighed too heavily on the scales of Lady Justice. Knoydart's tale is one of bitterness and hardship, a microcosm of the Highland's struggle between the rich and the dispossessed.

'Oh yes,' I added, 'People lived here but it was just too hard. Look at that hillside over there. Stone and lichen. You can't live on that.' There were quiet murmurs of agreement from men who knew all about subsistence farming on bare mountain sides. History often leaves indisputable evidence. Once people, a lot of people, lived here. Though whether in the twenty-first century we'd want to know the difference between sheer survival and a decent existence is a moot point.

'It looks like a good trout river anyway,' declared Ewen, and he was right. Fish were rising like an angler's dream. My brother, it should be realised, sees himself in the SAS – Special Angling Service (Trout Division).

'A couple of Peter Rosses, I reckon, would do the trick.' Right again, Bro', but not today. The packs were pulled on and the team trooped off over a mile of salt flats speckled with bog cotton to reach the edge of Loch Nevis. The route required regular leaps from grass-covered knolls over brown slimy mud. A ewe and two bleating lambs led the way like soulful heralds.

Behind us lay the stony bulk of Meall Bhasiter while on our left the rocky shoulder of Druim a Ghoirtein sloped down sharply to Loch Nevis. On the far shore was a green woolly cliff that rose directly into the

Overleaf. Left: **Dil, confident enough to pose on the wobbly bridge, looks cool.**
Right: **Gyan leads the boys down to Loch Nevis again through a gap in the mist.**

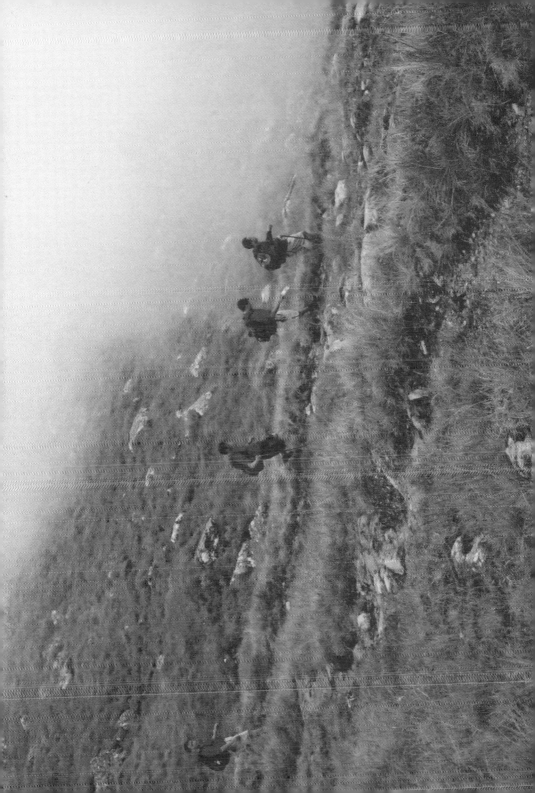

tumbled clouds which were now shot through with sunrays, promising better weather. The air had stilled into a silent cocoon, broken only by the harsh bleats of the leading lambs.

'Be careful here, guys. We're as far from help in the whole country as possible,' I pleaded as the lads stormed over the seaweed-strewn rocks that formed the spit before we turned left up to the east end of the loch.

After a couple of miles, goodbyes were said to the shore's shingle as a stiff switchback climb took us to the high hidden glen of Màm na Cloich Airde. It was this stony path that has supposedly broken the hearts of several famous hill-walkers and Munro-baggers. It's a full 750 feet straight into the sky and is one long rough-hewn staircase but, for reasons unknown, our little party, me included, chugged up like a small train, unworried. A waterfall fell in torrents just feet away, obliterating conversation. We found ourselves concentrating on the big boots of the man in front as they tirelessly clumped up the track. Gurkhas don't take particularly big strides, and often appear unhurried but are steady and remorseless with it. So it was today, and the climb was completed without pain. A new-found strength surged through my veins along with an unexpected sense of pleasure. Perhaps the gods were on our side. Let's face it, we had a whole Pantheon between us.

'That's fantastic!' exclaimed Dhal, his lean face creased, as he looked downwards. A patch of grass near the top invited it and we flung ourselves down for a moment's rest.

Below lay our last view of seawater for a week. The east end of Loch Nevis looked like a placid fjord, sixty feet deep. I had used a 1956 OS map and been baffled to read that the loch was ten feet at its deepest. In a fjordic sea loch? Surely not? Then I remembered: in those days, sea contours were measured in fathoms not feet. Nowadays they don't feature such fripperies at all, and one is obliged to buy Admiralty charts if one wants to know sea depth. Just as well I wasn't planning a seaborne invasion; we'd have had serious problems when the landing craft ramps flew down and our wee lads jumped into thirty feet of sea and not five.

The last Ice Age ended only 10,000 years ago and the two sea lochs Nevis and Hourn to the north, which both penetrate miles into the coastline, were created by glacial over-deepening of river valleys which existed before then. The land then slowly changed from tundra to woodland, mostly birch and hazel. Knoydart is still home to woodland flowers such as violets, wood anemones and wild hyacinth which tell us that these hillsides were until fairly recently covered by trees. The earliest signs of man in Scotland are Mesolithic and are found at Kinloch on Rum, dating back 6,600 years. It was Neolithic man that first began clearing the upland woods some 4,000 years ago.

Loch Nevis is sock-shaped, pinched at the waist and then bends out of sight to the sea. Just visible over the craggy back of Sgurr nam Meirleach on the left was the long silver surface of Loch Morar. A fresh water loch, it however plummets to over 1,000 feet: a deep mystery, furthered by the legend that it is home to a Nessie-like monster, Morag.

'We are doing fine, Neil?' asked Chandra, as he and Dil orientated the map, along with much fingering and frowning.

'Oh, yeah, we're doing great!' Everyone hummed proprietal approval of their view and happily glugged energy drinks.

'You know something,' said Ewen. 'I bet right now tons of guys are drinking these but we'll be the only people in the entire country that really need them!' Call me a puritan, but in previous walks I'd refused the Lucozade stuff, partly because of its price, and plumped for God's own mineral water. Silly really. The Almighty, as far as I know, has never specifically favoured any bottled water. This year, I was sinning and knocked back the isotonics like a mad alcoholic. As experts, we can report that the recuperative properties are truly amazing. The rush is almost instantaneous. Sweet, sweet, sugar for my baby maybe, but liquid glucose for my body, definitely.

As an anorak in these matters, it crossed my mind that 'iso' comes from the Greek meaning 'the same', as in isobars, but couldn't think who on the planet would be remotely impressed. I kept the sparkling fact to myself.

A finished climb has its own reward but we had not quite hit the halfway mark of the day's route, thanks to our late start. To our right, water poured from a gash in the rocky mountain wall like a long spurt of white blood, falling into a deep cleft which muffled the sound. I'm here for eternity, it seemed to say, while you're just passing through.

Remembering that we were probably on land owned by local boy made good, Sir Cameron Mackintosh, I took a few snaps to accompany a later begging letter. Yup, he sent a big cheque too! His house, Torran Albannach, Little Piece of Scotland, had just been burned down and the crime had reverberated around the land. Sir Cameron had showered charity on the area, even providing a swimming pool for Mallaig but to a malevolent few, his family house was a target. It wouldn't have been visible from where we were – it's on a southern point hidden by the loch's kink. Although I knew he owned 13,000 acres hereabouts I didn't know just where nor how big exactly is 13,000 acres. In fact, Sir Cameron owns everything from where his newly re-built castle stands all the way west to Mallaig. The impresario may be king of the West End, but he certainly enjoys dramatic settings. And in our book, and this, he's a star.

The landscape and weather took a theatrical turn. Treading our way along Màm na Cloich Airde the sun suddenly burst through, hitting us with a welcome warmth, lifting the clouds in long thin bars. Our red shirts blazed with colour as we stepped over the sheet rock. The wind fell away and our chatter carried on the still air like chirpy radio traffic. When I fell back to take a photo of the group set against the soaring backdrop, Chandra's walking commentary drifted over surreally clear as if speaking into my ear. We were in a long high-sided corridor of stone, above us only sky.

Gyan was chaffing that we weren't quite on the right path. 'Look, Gyan, at the moment there is no path but we know we're going in the right direction,' I said forcefully. I could feel an irritation rising, Gyan could be a bloody nuisance when he was like this. Dhal, recognising a well-known scenario, chuckled insubordinately.

'Is there a word for these?' asked Dil, pointing to the calm lochans, their water so clear that the few reeds could be seen right down to their base. I told him.

'And do these have a Nepali word?' I waved at a cairn.

'Stupa.'

Travellers had seen fit to build a series of cairns along the route, which told us plenty about the glen's weather. Without even discussing it the boys were tossing a stone or two on each passing cairn. Mountain boys, of course. Back home these would be further identified with strings of prayer flags, *dhoza*.

Ahead of us were the extraordinary 1,500 foot high walls of Garbh Chìoch Mòr, running north-south from Sgurr na Cìche (the peak of the breast), the highest point in Knoydart at 3,410 feet. This line of high mountains is properly called the Rough Bounds, na Garbh-Chrioachan, which marks the edge of Knoydart as immovably as the Pyrenees separate Spain from France. It looked like the Himalayas; perhaps that's why the boys were behaving as if they were at home.

Until now my imagination had dwelt only on how the Commandos had learned their skills here during World War II, but now *A Million Years BC* came to mind. There was practically no vegetation, only lifting smoky clouds and a stony vastness that was all encompassing. Had a dinosaur trundled into view I would not have been surprised. Had Rachel Welch any Scottish blood, I wondered?

When Bonnie Prince Charlie was on the run, aged just twenty-six, he had hidden in the Lochaber area and had even evaded the Redcoats in this very pass on the night of 19th July 1746. Had his hunters been our boys, they certainly wouldn't have been huddled round the watch fires by night. They'd have ambushed the fugitive and a thousand songs would have been rewritten.

'So why was he called 'Bonnie'?' asked Chandra.

'It means pretty. He was good-looking,' I said.

'Lucky would have been better,' commented Dil, suddenly laughing, 'Pretty Lucky!'

'Do you believe in luck, Neil?' I knew from experience that debating luck with Buddhists like Gyan was the foolish start to an appropriately endless cycle.

'Yes, of course I believe in luck. How else do I explain the successful careers of people I hate?'

There had been a series of Jacobite uprisings: 1689, 1708, 1715 and 1719. But the '45 was still called hereabouts Bliadhna Thearlaich (Charlie's Year). All were poorly led and organised. 1719 had actually seen the landing of Spanish troops at Kintail who were immediately captured but, embarrassingly, no-one wanted to pay their ransom.

Driving to Mallaig that morning we had passed the darkly-lit Glenfinnan Memorial, a stand-alone crenellated tower. Although more famous today for the nearby viaduct which was featured in *Harry Potter*, the Jacobite Standard had been raised there in a ceremony of hopeful theatricality but none of the principal chiefs 'came out'. Highlanders were understandably reluctant to become involved in a campaign which stood as little success as its ragged predecessors and which could cost them their heads and their children's inheritance. It surprises many, but more

Highland clans actively opposed Charlie than supported him. Macdonald of Clanranald, on to whose land he had stepped ashore, would not come out, nor would Macdonald of Sleat, nor MacLeod of Dunvegan. The latter is one of my heroes as one of the few clan chiefs who, trying to feed his tenants in the series of crop failures in the late 1700s, bankrupted himself. Most treated their clansman as redundant cattle and turfed them off the land if it involved financial gain.

The Gurkha Highlanders now stood in the prince's footsteps, the hopeful spirals of his trail giving little indication as to Charles Edward's eventual escape. Fleeing the bloody post-Culloden reprisals with £30,000 on his head, not a single Highlander so much as indicated his general location. Such unthinking loyalty, in the face of unremitting repression, has rarely been seen in world history. But these were the footprints we re-trod. Tearlach slipped through to Loch Luanie to the north and later, 20th September '46, made a happy rendezvous with the French frigate *L'Heureux.* 'Show me a King or Prince in Europe who could have borne the like, or a tenth part of it,' wrote Macdonald of Lochgarry. It was, as the French say, *tout finit par des chansons*, all over bar the songs, and songs there came aplenty. We're still writing them.

Now, 265 years later, the only salt on our soldiers' tails was time. We were approaching Glendessarry, training barracks to every World War II Commando, but there was little to remind us that here thousands of good men developed their stamina and learned to cut throats. Yet again, my sturdy colleagues could have shown the way. Had every Commando walked this lonely track? David Niven had been here, and his autobiography *The Moon's a Balloon* refers to Lochailort, beside the Glenfinnan monument where he was billeted.

The valley opened as we neared the day's end, and the colour green was re-introduced. Conifer plantations ran for miles on our right while the path became muddier and pitted with steep-sided puddles, where small patches of short grass stood alone like daft green toupees. By now I was beyond daintily crossing the torrential burns on steppingstones, and simply crashed in and waded across. The water was surprisingly warm.

We didn't know it, but the 15,000 acre Glendessarry estate was owned by one Sir Patrick Grant, founder and managing director of Grants of Dalvey, purveyors of luxury goods to Scottish and would-be Scottish gentlemen. In 1998 he had imposed a ban on the few walkers such as us from his summits in order to protect *his* valuable herds of red deer.

'Oh, look!' cooed Dil, not sure whether to shout or whisper.

Twelve fully-antlered stags trooped from the forest then sprang up the skyline to our immediate front, only yards away. Their flashing models' legs took them up the slope with a graceful fluidity. Then they stopped and looked down at us. Both groups eyed the other with mutual interest, rooted to the spot.

'Do they all have … ' asked Dil, miming antlers.

'Only the stags, the males,' replied Ewen.

'They're all men?' asked Surendra uncertainly.

A perfect evening light now glowed over the landscape as we crunched down the path which was broadening into a Land Rover track. As legs grew robotic, the west end of Loch Arkaig slowly came into view. Where was the pick up? The last hour of any job is the longest and tonight was no different.

At last. Only an old-fashioned five-bar gate separated us from the metalled road home and there, alleluia, was our van with driver Campbell McRoberts as delighted to see us as we him.

The first day's walk was over. We'd marched through some of the most exciting twenty miles that the Ordnance Survey has ever mapped, in about seven hours. The maps were practically brown with contours. The pace had occasionally risked disaster for a slow-footed *gora* (European) like me, as I jumped from rock to rock like an overweight Batman, but here we all were: home and happy.

The sun cast a special light on the backdrop as we posed for an end of day picture.

'Wow, Neil, you terrified us with your pre-march stuff about how shit today was going to be,' chided Ewen.

'It was fairly tough,' added Gyan, as if mediating. His name means 'Wisdom' and, by the gods, he liked to give us its benefit whenever he saw the need. It was the sort of thing you both laugh about, which, in turn, brings you closer.

'Yes, Neil Saheb, a good day?' asked Chandra, looking for confirmation.

Overleaf. *Left:* **Staff Sergeant Gyan Bahadur Tamang, Queen's Gurkha Signals, was always ready to give advice, even when it exasperated me!**
Right: **A million years BC? Any dinosaurs, guys? And does Rachel Welch have any Scottish blood?**

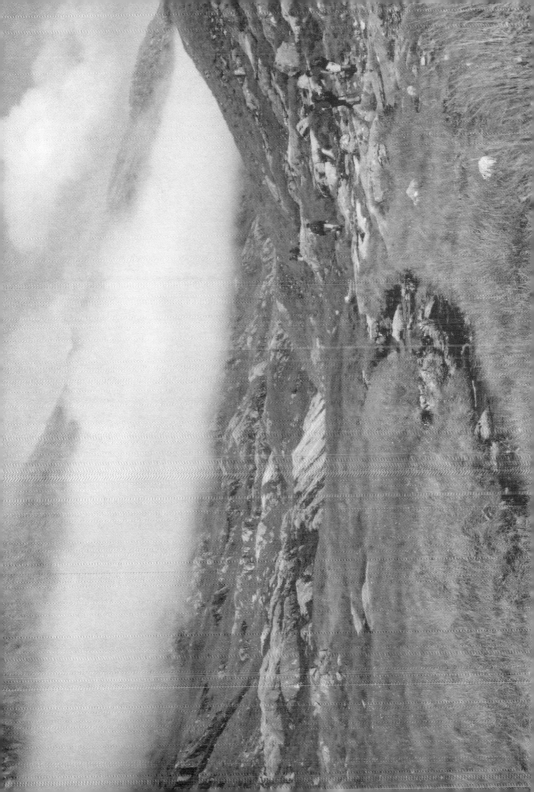

'*Ekdam ramro,*' I replied, 'Very good,' not quite sure whether a hot bath or a pint of lager was top priority. I was the cat that had got the cream, the mouse and the de luxe Kitekat. The boys were roundly happy – the greatest litmus test of all. My knees may have been slowly locking but my blood sang.

We drove down Loch Arkaig but, before turning off to our base at Spean Bridge, there loomed in the evening light the magnificent buffalo head of Ben Nevis. A real breath-taker, rearing into a Highland-blue sky with long white clouds trailing from its horns.

'Makes me feel proud!' I said.

'Why proud? You're not responsible!' grinned Gyan.

'No, I know, but this is my country and when I see it like this I feel good.'

Gyan muttered to himself, a son of mighty Everest itself, and unwilling to let a reference to mountain beauty go unchallenged.

Ben Nevis was apparently 'discovered' in 1892 by the Hopkinson family, which must have been a blessed relief to the locals, who'd been wondering what that big gap on the landscape must be. Although 'The Ben' is mainly pink granite, the uppermost parts and 2,000 foot cliffs are formed of bedded lava and other hard volcanic rocks which were intruded when a town-size block of granite collapsed and sank into a subterranean cauldron of molten rock some 400 million years ago.

Dhal, Gyan, Campbell, Ewen and I made a grave physiological error back at the hotel. While Surendra, Dil and Chandra charged into their baths, the senior party found themselves in stockinged feet at the bar of our temporary home, the Spean Bridge Hotel, a 17th Century coach house. My legs were now throbbing; any sensation, I reasoned, was a good sign. Sweat stiffened on my brow.

'Please allow me to get these,' offered the proprietor with the unforgettable name of Alex Ferguson. I wondered if his namesake is as generous when he meets Old Trafford customers.

It was here I decided that whatever the team did or did not do, we'd eat together every night. No bar snacks or snatched burgers. The family that eats together, stays together. Being in charge occasionally requires decision-making, and, although I'd established that the boys were on holiday, bonding was vital. This seems a small thing, but I was right. The

Opposite. **End of first day. My knees were locking but my heart sang.**

hotel provided a feast and everyone ate like Tudors, almost all on steak, with a gusto that Henry VIII himself would have recognised.

'The water for my bath,' said Chandra, 'was always brown.'

'Mmm,' I hummed, remembering the scalding gallons I'd allowed to pour down the plughole before realising that this was its natural colour.

'The water is peat-coloured here,' I explained as if the local water chief. 'It's what you get in the Highlands. It's what they make whisky from.' The subtle switch from bathwater to whisky was a bit much, and caused a moment of disbelief, but the strange fact was quietly absorbed like almost everything else the Gurkhas encounter in this country.

Later the boys were to be found in the hotel's Commando Bar at the pool table, taking on all comers. Final score: Scotland 4, Nepal 5. Bonhomie was further engendered by much drink. 'Sair heids the morn,' warned a local, but they hadn't sussed the Gurkhas.

'You're all dead!' chuckled Chandra, leaning over the table and potting a red. Surendra, behind him, nodded in confirmation. The local accent was difficult to decipher. About half the guys seemed to order 'Penicillin, please!' Can't be. Must be a pint of something – but what? Pint o'eighty shilling!

The magnificent seven had trekked across one of the wildest parts of Britain, taken the best and the worst summer weather that the Highlands can throw at anyone, marched across an area flooded with history and taken aboard its stories. Like a true Scot, I worried that we'd have to pay later for all these good times. Fate would balance it all out, and we'd pay for it, by God! The Gurkha philosophy is totally different: this is good, it will continue to be good, and, if it isn't, *jey hola, hola*, whatever will be, will be.

Yup, first day over and tomorrow a stroll. Gurkha Highlander looked good from where I was standing.

II

Loch Arkaig

~~~

It was Tuesday afternoon, three days before our start.

'Hi, Neil here. I called on his mobile. *'Tik chha?'*

'Oh, very fine. We are now at Darlington.'

'Darlington?' What are you doing in Darlington? You're supposed to be coming to Edinburgh tomorrow!'

'Yes, but we thought we'd come today.'

My mind swam. It would be no problem to house the three guys at my place, but it would have been nice to have had warning. What if I hadn't phoned?

'Look, I'll see you at the station in a couple of hours and then drive down to my flat.'

This was how my first meeting with Dil, Chandra and Surendra came about. Two hours later I was at Waverley Station awaiting my early birds. They were not just last to leave the train, but last by so much that I phoned to ask if they were still on it.

'Yes, we're getting off now.'

Three grinning lads in pressed shirts approached, carrying enormous amounts of luggage. None was above 5 foot 6 inches.

'Neil!' smiled Dil, handsome, stocky, neat. 'This is Surendra,' indicating a lean, shy colleague. 'And Chandra.'

'Ah, you're a Limbu,' I laughed, taking in his Tibetan features. 'You look like a Limbu!' His sparkling smile looked like some dental advert that you'd simply never believe on a poster. Had the guy Tippex-ed his teeth or what?

Let's not go on about it, but when three Gurkhas put themselves in your hands for a week, it's an unusual and privileged moment. I've not done anything particularly special in my life, so this was big stuff for me. The trusting, intelligent faces beamed nothing but goodwill and for the next few days they were *my* Gurkhas. We didn't know each other yet, but I knew that in a short period they would prove to be the best men I'd ever known and that it was only awkward that the moment hadn't yet arrived. And, yeah, Chandra must have Tippex-ed them.

In the taxi, Dil asked the curious question: 'So, what are we here for?' Curious because I'd explained everything to the corporal who should have been here in Dil's place. The day before he had been obliged to withdraw and clearly hadn't passed on some rather vital information. Chandra, too, was a last minute substitute.

'Well,' I said slowly. 'You're here for about ten days and you're part of a team that is going to walk 200 miles across the Highlands of Scotland, coast to coast.'

There were inclinations of the head which I knew were not knowing nods. 'It's a holiday,' I continued. 'We'll be staying in hotels or B&Bs and no guard duties!' Christ, I'm gushing.

At my flat, that old intercontinental stand-by, a pot of tea, was shared with a sense of ease. 'This,' declared Dil, sitting in *my* armchair, 'is just like home.' Supper at a Nepalese restaurant was garlic, chilli and chatty language lessons.

Dhal and Gyan swept in the following day, delighted to be back in Scotland. More chilli and garlic followed. Nepalese food is, like Nepal itself, part Indian, part Chinese, but with special ingredients of its own. Although I love it, my chilli radar (look-down mode) is always on – ever since that explosive day I nearly lost the top of my mouth when an entire *khursani,* chilli, slipped the dragnet. Strange to report, science has yet to discover a palliative that acts immediately in this context: a personal observation, my dears, learned the hard way.

Gyan took the remaining single bedroom, no questions asked, while Dhal slept on a sofa and Dil on a First World War camp bed, emblazoned with *British Expeditionary Force* which had once belonged to a great aunt who served as a nurse in Flanders.

The Gurkhas were not eligible for the Victoria Cross until 1915 but, as if to prove a point, almost immediately gained their first, going on to win a total of twenty-six. Thirteen of these were awarded to their British officers, which is strange, and suggests that the men inspire the officers as much as vice versa. Or perhaps the élan of the Gurkhas themselves attracted the Army's more adventurous officers. There isn't a class/race factor, either. Having read the many citations, I know that there was never a case where the British officer received a VC on behalf of his unit. It's not done that way. Everyone who ever won a VC earned it the hard way. Other famous regiments, such as the Royal Scots Greys, who won their first VC in the Crimea, only ever reached a total of three.

'Jes-us Cher-ist, guys,' greeted Campbell as we trooped up the hill into Edinburgh's New Town the next morning, 'What have you been eating?' Obviously the garlic and chilli were wafting downwind. Our man had just picked up the support van and was now, happily, able to take us anywhere within the UK.

In the store, Chandra stood stock still as he tried on a pair of walking boots, looking down at them gravely, as if disturbed.

'Ramro, eh?' I queried. There was no reply. Puzzled, I asked: 'Gyan, what's wrong here?' There was a rapid exchange in Nepali.

'His boots are too thin,' explained Gyan, holding his palms nearly together.

'Well, get him another pair!'

'He thinks these are gifts from you, Neil, and doesn't want to offend by asking for another pair.'

'Chandra, get yourself boots that fit properly, or I *will* be offended.'

The lad gave a quick shrug of embarrassment and relief, but reached for other boots. This was why Gyan was with us. Not only as the Senior NCO but, as in all Gurkha units, to act as liaison between the British leader and the men whenever cultural problems arose. The shop's early morning staff had rarely had an eight-man group walk in, demanding boots, shorts and thirty-two pairs of heavy duty socks, but were delighted to see us. 'We give a 10% discount to members of the Forces and the police. Usually we ask for ID,' explained the manager, 'But I don't think that's necessary in your case!'

When the warriors left, fully and properly accoutred, the staff had become friends and I suspected we were going to be asked to 'keep in touch'. Frankly, I was delighted and relieved that my credit card had operated without the usual declamations as to the failings and follies of the banking system. So much so that I allowed Gyan to buy his blasted long trousers in the moment of triumph. I made a mental note, though: learn the Nepali for 'make sure your boots fit.'

At Tesco, shoppers kept asking if the boys were going to enjoy the Tattoo. A pre-ordered trolley of energy drinks in wee bags and bottles of mineral water awaited but our main concern was grabbing fruit and chocolate snacks. At last, we reached the checkout like part of one big, healthy, mixed-race family where only the men do the shopping.

'Where's the water trolley?'

'Don't know.'

'Chandra took it to the van.'

'What! We haven't paid for it!'

Chandra was found in the car park carefully loading the van with sixty-four bottles of Highland Spring. I think the security guard was more embarrassed than me – especially as Tesco had given us a 10% discount as well as £10 off the total bill. Chandra, who had presumed that pre-ordered meant prepaid, was mortified. He had been in a position where someone could have accused him of theft, and was slow to see the funny side. 'Infantry!' grinned Gyan and Dhal.

Gyan divided out the first aid kit: ankle support, knee support and so forth. 'And a stomach support for you, Neil?' poking the great Griffiths belly. Ouch!

'That's not fat, that's solid muscle. I've been bulking up for this!'

So here we are at Loch Arkaig on another grey morning. Whatever happened to the cloudless evening of yesterday? Answer: the Atlantic has moved in. Campbell had driven us back to where we'd finished the night before, by the five-barred gate at the west end of the loch. It was a sick-making drive down a swooping single track with fourteen miles of dark water on one side and anonymous hillside on the other.

How were we going to walk this without dying of boredom? How was morale going to cope? Spending several hours moving east along miles of undulating tarmac was not on par with conquering the mighty heights of the Highlands but there was no other route.

'Listen, guys.' I explained, 'Today is twenty miles along this road until we hit the hotel at Spean Bridge. It's not what we're here for but it has to be done.'

The subtext was that this was an easy stroll, not mountaineering, but a necessary day of soldiering which would see another section of the route completed. No one seemed bothered. I wore trainers and, God, we walked and walked, past little farm houses and smaller cottages, but always on the right was the 300 foot dark depths of Loch Arkaig.

'On my first visit to Scotland,' started Dil, 'I got out of the train at Newcastle thinking it was Edinburgh. The next day a lady told me I was in the wrong town.'

There were roars of laughter. 'Newcastle? What made you get off there?'

Dil shrugged. 'I knew Edinburgh had a castle so when I saw Newcastle ... '

'Wha-hay, bonny lad, you're in the wrong toon!' I giggled.

Dil was good at lifting spirits. While Surendra was often gravely serious, he would chuckle loudly at Chandra's Nepali monologue. Our Moon Boy was a natural joker, if not a linguist.

'I expect he'll go far,' I said of Chandra as an aside to Gyan, who instantly switched to Senior NCO role, and added that one couldn't be certain at this stage, eighteen months since joining.

When we stopped the guys pulled off their boots and paddled as if this were a proper holiday. The loch had witnessed other holidaymakers; in 1873 Queen Victoria, John Brown and other royal attendants had visited as part of Her Majesty's famous Jacobite tour. Cameron of Lochiel, in full Highland fig, had greeted her at his Anchnacarry seat at the east end of the loch. Like Cluny MacPherson, who had dogged the queen's travels, Lochiel was the descendant of a die-hard Jacobite who had nearly toppled Victoria's forbears. 'Stuart blood runs in my veins,' she had told him. We can only guess what Charles Edward would have made of it. And what would have been the response had someone at Culloden predicted that in a couple of hundred years a Cameron of Locheil would open the visitors' centre? I leave that one to you. Remember this, if you want to hear God laugh, tell him about your plans for the future.

Interestingly, Sir William MacPherson of Cluny is now an Establishment figure too, and recently completed the inquiry into the death of Stephen Lawrence. Had all Culloden losers done well for themselves? How the fallen are mighty.

Overleaf: *Left:* **Loch Arkaig. When there was water, it was impossible to stop the boys paddling.**
Right: **Ewen pretending to enjoy himself in zero visibility.**

The royal party had been taken up the loch in a small steamship, admiring the then thick oak forests that grew on both sides; the south was for deer and the north for sheep, although Lochiel commented that the oaks were but weeds and sold the lot soon after. Today the hills are bare, bar a few conifer plantations on the south side. This too has a link with history, for it was where Bonnie Prince Charlie briefly met French officers in the summer of '46 to plan his escape.

Today though it was up to us Gurkha Highlanders to plod on until we at last reached our lunch spot, having completed the length of the blessed loch. Even here, it was not a good day. Squadrons of midges formed up like circling fighters. Remember the RAF's Big Wing? This was it in miniature, albeit with far greater numbers. For those of you who have never been subject to the great Caledonian midge, I have to tell you, you're an innocent abroad, and lucky, very lucky.

'I'm going up there,' said Gyan, swotting and slapping, pointing to a waterfall. No one will ever know what Gyan saw or experienced at the falls, but lunch was memorable for all the wrong reasons. Soon we found ourselves on a long dark road, as if from a German fairy tale: huge pines on either side hiding the sun, and deep wet moss below. I stopped for a pee and counted four frogs. Only later did I learn that this was called The Dark Mile, on account of Lochiel's fatal decision to leave Achnacarry along this route, taking 800 clansmen to support Prince Charlie. Although against his better judgement, he felt obliged to do so, and his vital support made the whole '45 possible.

Dhal, Gyan and Dil had the muscle-bound legs that perhaps a cartoonist would invent, complete with a dimple above the knee created by the wrapping and crossing of their immense quads, while their calves bulged with hard-worked muscle. The next anatomist to write a text could do worse than phone the Brigade of Gurkhas before depicting the lower limbs section. Surendra's were more European-looking but Chandra's were practically thin, like those of a colt. As I watched, his little Limbu legs suddenly tore up the slope to a promontory so that, to great hoots from Gyan and Surendra, he could mime diving over us. The energy was as unremarked as it was remarkable. Even on a quiet day, I was being shown up.

Before we crossed the Caledonian Canal our only entertainment had been watching an angler land a trout on Loch Lochy. We had unthinkingly crept up behind him and the first he knew of our presence was the sight of several Nepalese heads peering over his shoulder from the undergrowth. Upon reflection, he was quite calm.

Ben Nevis loomed above us and I giggled to myself. The editor of the hillwalking magazine, *Trail*, had recently apologised after his publication had printed an incorrect route down Ben Nevis. The directions, designed to help walkers in poor visibility, would have led them over a cliff. Guy Proctor said he was 'gutted' by the error (and the use of cliché), but thought readers would notice. He did not, however, specify at what point this might happen.

The surrounding trees were no less tightly spaced, and hid most views, but featured a large range of species, including several lofty Douglas firs, named after the Scottish botanist, David Douglas, who first brought them back from the Pacific North West in the 1820s. He was also the damn fool responsible for introducing the sitka spruce.

Four miles on and we could see the proud clump of bronze that is the Spean Bridge Commando Memorial. The larger-than-life figures of three Commandos beneath their woollen caps with weapons slung, looked brave, tough and evocative. Their pose is one of unity and purpose, but not of belligerence. The sculptor reckoned, surprisingly, that the dimensions were easier to work with than life-size. His achievement is a towering memorial which obliges visitors to raise their eyes – a psychologically powerful act – to absorb the Commandos who look out at the equally rugged countryside to Ben Nevis, ten miles away over the Leanachan Forest. It is a sensational location and an extraordinary tribute. Our host at the Spean Bridge Hotel told us that he had never passed it in daylight hours without spotting a visitor. Today there were a couple of bus loads staring at the three giants, everyone lost in reverie.

A Royal Marine friend assured me that the Corps always sends a troop from 45 Commando at *HMS Condor*, Arbroath, on Remembrance Sunday, when the snow-topped mountains add to the sense of wilderness and sadness.

Gurkhas revere soldier heroes (it's only recently that they've been part of the Cenotaph parade in Whitehall) and were quietly pleased to see that the tradition was so strong here.

'Gyan, are your feet okay?' I asked.

'Yes, just a bit sore with all this road walking.'

'You can hop in the van if it's a problem.'

'No, I'm okay.'

We walked the two miles to our hotel, arriving at about 5 p.m., with Gyan limping at a pitiful pace which boded ill for the morn.

'Are you sure you're okay?'

'Yeah, just sore.'

No one wanted to say anything because Gyan had endured blister agonies on our 340-kilometre Southern Upland Way trek the year before and had been forced to take a couple of days off. The same clenched teeth were back. My heart sank. Gurkhas traditionally ignore physical impediments, such as a missing leg or two, to fulfil an objective, but I was obliged to balance this with the possibility of returning a Gurkha to his unit with a lasting injury.

'Oh well, we're home now,' I said to Ewen.

'See how he is tomorrow,' added Dhal, a confidant whose judgement we all trusted.

Supper was a repeat of the beano blow-out of the night before where the boys wanted heaps of food, and nothing but the best. The hotel was now becoming home and less a new experience. Manikins in Commando gear posed in every corridor and framed pictures of wartime Commando training filled the walls as if this were a strange backwater military mess. There was no feel of luxury, the carpets were worn and old fashioned but it exuded a comfort not associated with the modern chic chain hotels. This place had individuality.

'Tomorrow I'll show you my private Commando museum,' promised Alex Ferguson, an offer rarely heard in Holiday Inns.

They even knew our order at the bar where a beautiful brunette poured the pints. The lads were extraordinarily interested in her social life and asked many times if she were married. Let's be honest, they weren't alone in asking.

It must have been cooler that night, for we all wore our navy blue sweatshirts. Both Chandra and Surendra were missing the striking crossed

Opposite. **Near Loch Lochy. The team prepares to move off looking both fresh and thoughtful.**

Overleaf. *Left:* **Dill in serious mode**.

Right: **Ewen enjoying sunshine.**

kukris above the words 'Gurkha Highlander' embroidered on the left. Why were they wearing the shirts back to front, and how had they been so dim as not to notice? Then it dawned on me: these were blank sweatshirts and this suddenly explained why I had two properly embroidered extra ones in my room. The suppliers had mucked up! What I thought were free gifts were an error. The two shirts in my luggage could no longer be surprise gifts for future benefactors: they belonged to these two. I ran back to my room.

'Sorry about that guys!' I tossed the new shirts at them. They immediately pulled them on, grinning like kids with a new, flash outfit.

An Englishman tapped me on the shoulder and asked if his youngsters could be photographed with our lads. Embarrassed that he had asked me, I got as far as, 'Well, of course ... ' before the big-eyed children were instantly surrounded by our lot, Kodak smiles on full beam, like obedient models. The kids dissolved into giggles, all delighted to be part of such an uncomplicated moment of British-Gurkha fraternity.

The waitress gave me a message. 'Excuse me. I've got to give some interviews to the BBC,' I announced as if this were some terrible but inevitable chore to be expected by public figures like wirsel. The deed was done from a phone in the residents' lounge and eventually hit the starry airwaves of BBC Highland and BBC Aberdeen. I was truly inept, missing out all the important stuff but sounding enthusiastic. However, as they say, all publicity is good publicity.

A large German family was witness to my call, drinking coffee and discussing their day. I like Germans and introduced myself. What would they make of all this? I'm with a group of soldiers and staying in a hotel that practically shouted 'Germans, raus!'

Born in Edinburgh, baptised in Luneburg, brought up in Minden, Berlin, Gutersloh and Nord Rhein Westphalia, I had worked in the Moselle vineyards and nearly married a tall blonde daughter of Heidelberg. Germany is part of my past and of me. I love the country and am only sad that nearly all my compatriots don't know it at all.

They were genteel Bavarians who were either blind to the military paraphernalia of the hotel or considered it normal.

'Ah, Sie sind der Mann aus Nepal?' You're the man from Nepal, said the mother, nodding.

'No, I'm just their friend. *Nein, Ich bin gerade ihrer Freund.'* German is the perfect language for affirmatives.

The evening sky was cloudless and still unfeasibly light, but the air bore a delicious freshness that lifted the lungs. Retrieving our stiffly dried Knoydart socks from a dryingroom outhouse, we retired to sleep in the dreamless depths known only to the tired, fit and happy.

III

To Corrour Station

~~~

Sunday morning at eight saw us tramping out of the hotel, past the time-capsule Hornby railway station, and along the silent tree-lined road east, on the south side of the Spean. Where it could, the sun sliced through the sycamores and hit us with shafts of brilliance. The few cottages looked wearily in need of investment while every curtain was sleepily drawn shut.

Dil, ever keen to learn, asked: 'So, Scotland is not independent but has its own parliament. How is that possible?'

'Well, we have, like, a First Minister who is a sort of a prime minister, except he's not. Fortunately they're both in the same party, except they have slightly different policies. There's no second chamber, no ministry of defence, no foreign office, no department of social security and no treasury.'

'Ah,' exhaled Dil. 'But taxes?'

'Well, theoretically they can fix some taxes, but they don't.' Really, Donald Dewar should have been subject to all this, preferably on a Sunday morning. The first time I met Mr Dewar was at the Scottish Office at Whitehall. I was passing an office in the basement where I saw the then Secretary of State talking to his computer in an over-animated way. 'He's cracked,' I thought. It was only later I realised he was in video conference.

Our little family turned off the road and trudged south up a stony track through firs and suddenly the view opened into a Cinema Scope landscape that was near alpine. Ahead lay bright green meadows while the horizon was ripped by the saw-toothed peaks of the Grey Corries, a row of eight mountains each over a thousand metres. Clouds rose from them like a steam bath while the sunlight tightened our eyes. Unbelievably, a squall was coming from the west. Of course, we're in Scotland.

To the left lay a deep green forest clinging round a notch in the skyline which was the pass to which we were headed. This is what Sunday mornings are for.

'Phew, malai garmi bhayo! I'm hot,' I exclaimed, as the guys hit a pace that had me gasping. The big boots crunched on the stone with an unremitting aggression. The squall had disappeared and we were on the move. We charged through Leanachan Forest, as if in a race, up some rather horrible contours for two miles. Eventually we came to the edge and stopped for water, grinning at each other as if this were all one big hoot.

'Well, that was a bit of a bastard,' I said.

'Yeah,' agreed Dil, almost pensively, as Chandra grinned silently. Gurkhas have a nasty game, I suspect, of pretending to each other that long slow climbs must not feature on the dial, and that even to acknowledge their existence is a sign of hilarious weakness. My suspicions, first awakened in Knoydart, were now confirmed as the whole team thrust forward without comment. This had been pure Gurkha showmanship.

We had roared past a couple of skinny pensioners in all the gear, complete with ski sticks. You know the type, bean-eating scarecrows with plaited grey hair and love beads looking for a tree to hug.

'Those sticks, Neil, can take 30% of the strain off your knees,' commented Ewen.

The prospect of having less painful knees was tempting, but how can I, friend of the Gurkhas, Lord of the Mountains, possibly be seen with the complete Saga stuff? I'd rather die of joint rot than be seen using the same gear as an old lady. The only physical solution was to lose weight, i.e. never drink lager ever again. Well, that's clearly quite impossible.

Surendra squinted up at the next stage, one of huge badly eroded hillsides with a Land Rover track wending its way like a spinal cord between vast muscular shoulders. 'The route levels out now,' announced Dil, looking up from the map.

Overleaf. *Left*: **The team's rock, Gyan, looking unusually tired in the rain and wind**
Right: **Leaving Spean Bridge, waterproof covers over packs and heading for the pass on the left of picture.**
Next page. **Corrour Station. Thanks to ScotRail we had free return tickets to Spean Bridge**

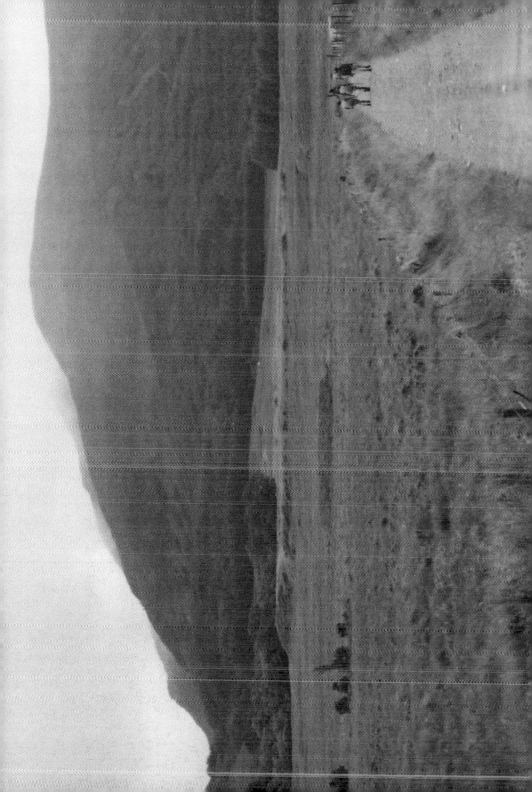

'Was that an old railway?' asked Gyan, referring to a track we had crossed before the forest.

'Yeah, I read in a magazine that about a hundred years ago some millionaire built a country house up here and then laid on a private railway from way over there,' I pointed eastwards, 'So that his guests could arrive by train. Silly bugger. He must have gone bust pretty quickly with that kind of expenditure.' The track looked as if it had been gone for about a hundred years.

'But it's good, isn't it, Neil, that people built railways wherever they wanted?' countered Dil, awestruck by the idea.

'Oh yes, the rich then were very rich.' The tracks' remains were now but a row of small grey wooden sleepers, but you had to wonder at the dreams and wealth of the man who had paid for them. The Highlands were, and are still, home to the visitations of extraordinary individuals – as we were to see.

It was like learning that the Santa doesn't exist when I learned the truth about the track; the dismantled tramway runs from the northern tip of Loch Treig across to the aluminium works at Fort William and was built to assist with the construction of the tunnel that connects the two. Well, I didn't even know that a tunnel existed. Shame really, I liked the eccentric millionaire story much better.

The sun shone directly into our eyes as we headed up what was perhaps the only glen in the OS without a name, with the enormous Cruach Innse on our left and a range topped by Stob Coire na Ceannain, 1,123 metres, to our right clad in the first heather we'd seen. They were treeless and imposing and part of me wanted to remember them forever. I had told the BBC how difficult it was to pronounce the Gaelic names, but I could translate most into Nepali or English, and the boys were eager to learn.

'Let's stop here,' said Ewen.

There was a bridge over the unnamed burn that bubbled down to Spean behind us. The sun was out and I was walking through a beautiful part of my homeland with a bunch of Gurkhas. Could life get any better?

The bonus was that we were counting off the miles and not only was it not hurting, but it was uplifting, and edging towards joyous. The glen was silent and blissfully uninhabited. The phrase 'walking on air' took on a new meaning; this was heaven. If that seems extreme, I have to tell you, it was.

'You know, Ewen, even if I photographed this, it simply wouldn't capture this moment,' I said. The air was fresh and we were in high spirits.

'Mars minibars!' grinned Dhal. 'How much you think they pay us to do an advert like this?' He waved at the high green hills. 'Millions!' and cackled to himself.

The long glen reached its watershed at exactly 500 metres before falling away to become the Lairig Leacach. The route had risen 420 metres from Spean Bridge and we now stood at half a kilometre in the sky. The stobs and sgurrs were only 400 metres above but their dimensions, rolling away from us, gave them a majestic unassailability. We had a new burn on our left, the Allt na Lairige, which ran ahead for five miles to Loch Treig through thick heather in a series of sparkling waterfalls. The Almighty doesn't skimp.

We stopped where the new glen broadened slightly, just before the route divides and goes westwards to the Grey Corries on our right. The team was headed straight on but sat down by a bothy to chat to three walkers. Unfortunately, one took it upon himself to ask in the crudest terms about the assassination of the Nepalese royal family.

'He asked me,' spat Dhal later, 'if we believed it was an accident. Does he think we're all idiots?'

No matter how indignant had been the Gurkha reaction, I noticed that not one of them had so much as evinced irritation during the conversation. Their natural good manners meant that our hill-walkers were completely unaware of the offence and happily asked us to form up for a photo. Be bloody careful, I thought to myself, not to do the same. I thought I knew these guys but occasionally I realised how different they were. A recent guide book published in Nepal describes Dil's clan, the Rais, 'as a gentle people but also said to have a quick temper and are known to be fast with a kukri without caring too much about the consequences.' Not bad for a gentle people, eh?

The assassination comment had angered everyone, but we were further annoyed to discover some recently dumped compo (army tinned food) and a live .762 round. Unanimously, the TA was blamed, but the guilt was shared. I was suddenly back in the Army.

The sun still burned, leaving black shadows behind us, and having trooped through wet peat we hit a narrow sheep-track of dry stone between calf-high heather which took us in the right direction.

'Is this the right path?' asked Ewen. 'We should be down by the river.'

'Yeah, we're too high but the path down there must be following all those re-entrants,' I commented. We couldn't see the correct path but were following the river, albeit on a higher track.

'We're on the wrong route,' announced Gyan, like some Nepalese headmaster, voice heavy with accusation. The group stopped to fix our spot, huddled round the battered map.

'We should be down there,' repeated Gyan.

'Yes, but look at it. Marshy and goes in and out following the riverside.'

'We're in the wrong place,' he rebutted.

Taking a deep breath, I decided: 'We keep going on this path until we reach that bit over there,' pointing to the skyline, 'Then we'll see if the right path is visible and head down towards it. We're surrounded by heather here.'

It seemed we were agreed but moments later Gyan not only repeated his conviction that we were on the wrong route but added that we were now veering right, up to the Grey Corries.

I admit it. I lost it. 'Kali, we know we're on the wrong route but we just agreed that we'll go down to the right path when a route there is clear.'

He started giggling that I'd called him Kali but repeated, 'We're on the wrong route.'

Thoroughly annoyed by now that he and he alone was buggering up the day, I decided, that in the face of such intransigence, acquiescence would be no bad thing. But wasn't this mutiny?

'Okay, let's head down to the river right now!' I thought of pushing Gyan, or stamping my little plimsole but thought better of it. Funnily enough, Gyan was right and we slipped and slid down the dry heather in

Overleaf. *Left:* **Bridge of Thighs: Dhal and Chandra take time out on the way to Loch Treig.**
Right: **Ewen on the way to Loch Treig. Note the heavily eroded hillsides.**
Next page: **Forgot we're dealing with soldiers? Surendra with 84 mm Carl Gustav anti-tank weapon.**

a matter of minutes, through pockets of grass and young bracken. There was one tricky burn to negotiate which sluiced across pink-orange sheet rock but it took perhaps ten minutes to be standing on the correct path.

I had not been wrong but Gyan's stubborn insistence as to when we switched paths was bloody infuriating. Nevertheless, I loudly announced how Gyan was right – very graciously, I thought. To add, literally, injury, I twisted my ankle in the long stuff and was convinced it was partly Gyan's fault but didn't dare announce the fact.

'Not exactly your finest hour, Neil!' chirruped my brother.

'I thought you were going to smack his mouth,' added Dhal, disappointed (and where did you, Dhal, learn such a colloquialism?). In fact, this had been an argument between friends. Only family and friends actually go at each other; enemies mutter.

The glen to Loch Treig unfolded in lonely beauty. A high ridge to our right held on to a pure white shard of cloud, as if playing. The mountains slept, almost breathing, their stony ribs bleeding cascades of crystal while the lush breeze blew into our happy lungs.

Eventually, a stony gorge fell to our right, fretted with tall, slim pines. We stopped above it like pilgrims. Tiny scraps of cloud, like white prayer flags, blew through the heavens above us.

So enchanting was the moment that no one spoke. Minutes later we were stepping through a cleuch, a narrow ravine through grey cliffs, down naturally-made steps, the path apparently from some Arthurian tale. Tall walls rose above us, but the route magically invited us through to an Arcadian scene of spellbinding tranquillity. A trout burn with tight green grass borders took us through a rural set so idyllic that my mind flew to children's books and, embarrassingly, *The Wooden Tops*.

If it were possible to stop and camp here, I swear that within a week we'd have ended up as a bunch of Wordsworths. However, seven days of unbroken glorious summer are rare hereabouts and as realists who knew all about the poverty that goes with mountain beauty, the Gurkhas pushed on.

A stony path took us from this dreamy paradise to the southern end of Loch Treig, a vast deep loch hemmed by monstrous hills. Like most Highland lochs, it was narrow, about seven miles long, and filled a valley scoured deep in a forgotten Ice Age.

At our end stood a vacant stone-built house, its windows staring out like the empty sockets of a blinded soldier. Surprisingly, the slates were in good condition and a new Scottish saltire snapped in the wind above them.

'We've got to cross the river on a bridge round the back of that,' I explained.

The boys clambered over long-abandoned sheep pens, their dry pine grey with age, until we came to what could have been the most dangerous river crossing of our whole trip. Two sturdy 50 foot girders, as if snaffled from some engineering project, lay across a hundred foot gorge. Between the rusting metal were solid ancient planks, like sleepers. There were no fripperies such as railings and the drop was a shocker.

Below dashed the Abhainn Rath over van-size blocks of stone, the water rushing from the Mamore Forest to our east where it shares a source with the hurtling Water of Nevis, one of the country's great watersheds, whose gorge is often compared to the Himalayas themselves. I understood in a flash the urge to harness these torrents that must have inspired the creators of the North of Scotland Hydro-Electric Board. I'll never read the label 'Highland Spring' with the same blankness ever again.

'It's perfectly safe,' said Ewen, 'They probably take tractors over it.'

'They *used* to!' said Gyan knowingly.

My brother was right. It was rock solid. Had it not been, our party would now be lost corpses with stoved-in skulls somewhere under Loch Treig.

Rejoining the stony loch-side path, we stopped for lunch only to be bothered by clegs, horseflies. We had been moving too fast for comfort and my knees were hurting as if I'd fallen heavily on to concrete. There was a reason for our speed.

'When we get there you are buying the beers', said Dil over a chicken sandwich.

'Becks for me,' added Chandra, 'Or maybe a Holsten.'

Christ, not exactly simple hillboys, are they, I thought. 'We should get to the station about an hour before the train arrives. Plenty of time for a beer.'

The ales in question were, we believed, lined up at the bar of Corrour Station, perhaps the strangest railway stop in Britain. It has no adjacent roads and the investors in the West Highland Railway must have been at their daftest when they backed its construction.

On the edge of Rannoch Moor, 'A wearier-looking desert man never saw,' (Robert Louis Stevenson, *Kidnapped*) Corrour Station stands as testimony to the Victorians' belief in the unfailing return on rail. The inaugural train of the WHL was only in 1894 and packed with some of the country's most hopeful investors. They must have looked at the uninhabited landscape and wondered where all the passengers would come from. They're still wondering. Corrour Station, without even access roads, was the very zenith of their optimism.

'We're walking down to Corrour Station,' we'd told guys in the Commando Bar. 'Then coming back to Spean Bridge.'

'Oh, they've just opened a bistro there. You'll get good food. A young couple, I believe.'

This was the place made famous in *Trainspotting* for Renton's soliloquy: 'It's shite being Scottish. We're the lowest of the low. The scum of the f****** earth.' I fancied that had we run into this troop there might have been war but my initial planning had been stymied by the fact that we needed transport from the station back to Spean Bridge. The map showed private roads which were known to be locked and that the landowner, Hans Rausing, the 6'8" Tetra Pak billionaire, was hardly going to be standing smiling with keys at every gate for our minivan.

Phoning John Yellowlees, ScotRail's press officer, I asked the obvious: 'How does your staff get to work every day at Corrour Station?'

'By train, Neil.' No kidding.

John not only sent me return tickets free of charge, he included a publication about the WHL, booked our seats and made sure the staff knew all about us. Thanks, John.

Hence today, we not only had a train to catch but a beer to sink. A stiff climb up to the railway track was tackled at the clatter. The whole thing looked straight out of *Railway Modeller Monthly*. The landscape was surreally neat, like one of those 1950s over-rich colour postcards that would have you believe that everywhere in Scotland was practically the Garden of Eden and set beneath a single tone sky of unfeasible blueness. Whatever happened to those cards? Remember when people used to send them from Saltcoats and Kirkcaldy – which had apparently been shifted to the Mediterranean?

The lovely, lonely station came slowly into view on the plateau, as our path degenerated into black mud and clapped-out duckboards. An Airfix signal box stood beside the fabled bistro. Exposed, a hot, dry wind blew dust in our nostrils as if this were Texas crossed with a huge peat moor. A spinning windmill set high above completed the scene.

'The bar's closed,' announced Dhal through gritted teeth. In fact, it had been closed for months. So much for local advice. A thirsty hour beckoned. Kit was dumped in a shelter, notices were read, the low horizons scanned. There's bog all to do at Corrour, take it from me. There was a joke about the Gurkha Welfare Trust having been given a platform to promote itself, but no one laughed.

'Neil, Chandra's in trouble with his knee,' advised Gyan

I strapped up Chandra's right knee with a long crepe bandage (which I never got back). He was in semi-serious pain, and I advised rest and hot bathing, but there was no way he was going with us the next day. There were mutters of disappointment but to return an injured Gurkha to his unit was beyond consideration. These fundraising walks depend on the goodwill of the British Brigade of Gurkhas supplying us with serving soldiers. If it were known that they frequently, or at all, entailed casualties foolishly brought about, it would be the end of them.

'Sorry, Chandra. You may be out for two days, but you won't be Returned To Unit.' Being RTU-ed, as it's called, is a badge of shame for all soldiers on a course or exercise. 'You'll stay with Campbell tomorrow and if there's no improvement you'll see a doctor.' Gyan was interpreting; no nuance was to be misunderstood.

There was that deadpan stare at the ground that I knew meant deep disappointment. This was an old injury, which had recurred on the march up from the loch.

'It was a happening,' said Chandra grimly, 'waiting to accident.'

Dear God, where *do* they learn these phrases? This was a holiday, I had stressed. Enjoy yourself. I had become aware that his happy personality was important to the group too. Chandra was of us, and would remain that way.

The train came, quiet and unintrusive, almost slipping over the horizon. The hot atmosphere inside the carriages took us by surprise, as

Opposite: **First aid for Chandra.**

did the Sunday papers which reminded us that the world was continuing out there, somewhere.

Dil and Surendra found themselves surrounded by young Glaswegians. 'You're Bobby Petta, aren't you?' they asked.

'Yes,' nodded Dil, as if shyly acknowledging he was indeed the Celtic football star.

'So why are you here?'

'Aren't you playing at Ryan Giggs's testimonial tomorrow?'

'Ah,' replied our man, unfazed. 'That's tomorrow, today is for Scotland.' Quite how a man with Gurkha, literally, written all over him could get away with such a porkie defeats me. But Gurkhas are great with kids, and both sides knew they were having a laugh.

The mighty Loch Treig, whose name means Loch Desolation (and is roundly unfair), disappeared to our left, allowing us to gaze at the rounded ruggedness of Stob Coire Easain, 1,116 metres, behind it, with the wistfulness and wisdom of proper hillmen.

The train passed through the hamlet of Fersit, home to Rudolf Hess for most of World War II, and through villages with wonderful Highland names like Tulloch and Roybridge, gladed with summer birch, before pulling into Spean Bridge.

The day was far from over. Campbell, arms folded over his crested red shirt, stood before the van into which we trooped and headed for the Commando Memorial. This was for the one moment when we stopped and paid attention to our trek's other raison d'être: not just raising funds for the 12,000 surviving wartime Gurkhas but also to honour the memory of those that fell in battle. The British-Gurkha relationship is much more than a friendship society; it is one of soldiers fighting alongside each other. Men, many men, died forging these bonds of blood and today we were going to remember them. A special wreath had been produced in the Lady Haig Poppy Factory, Edinburgh, with crossed kukris set against RGR colours. The attached dedication read: 'From mountain men to mountain men, in sad remembrance and proud affinity' and was signed by the whole team.

A Buddhist scripture, the Mahaparininirvana, states: 'A stupa should be erected at the crossroads for the tathagata [somebody who has attained a higher status]. And whoever lays a wreath or colours there with a devout heart will reap benefit and happiness for a long time.'

The sky was blue and distant. We stood in single line with a large respectful crowd watching.

'Squad! Squad, shun!' I said softly.

Gyan moved forward over the stone flags and laid our wreath. There was a brief silence, broken by the moans of Dhal's pipes which then sprang into a blood-searing Flowers o' the Forest – written for Flodden and played by Scots where'ere they grieve. The lament rose and fell as we stood proudly, sadly. A hundred people froze around us. Then it was over. No clapping. It was majestic, profound, uplifting and heart-rending.

'That was excellent,' I said quietly to Dhal, who looked twice the man he had been minutes before.

Then the press photographers took their pictures. It was unusual that they held off during our little ceremony, but I think I can guess why. The group pictures showed the happiest, proudest bunch ever caught on film. We had indeed reaped benefit and happiness.

Overleaf. *Left:* Spean Bridge Commando Memorial with the happiest, proudest bunch on film.
Right: Sergeant Dhal Bahadur Saki, our piper, looking imperturbable and not to be meddled with.

IV

To Dalwhinnie

~~~

The wind was cold and the grey skies low as we trooped off the little train. Corrour was at its summer bleakest, despite the sunlit July stillness we'd left at Spean Bridge. The green waterproof jackets were zipped up over blue sweatshirts as the team trundled along the dry mud road past a silver Loch Ossian. It was downright nippy.

'This isn't,' groaned Dhal, 'what the brochures promised.'

Deep heather, flecked with gorse, lay to our sides while ahead stood three miles of conifer plantation. Chandra wasn't with us and Surendra, as the only rifleman, was tending to walk by himself. Perhaps I was wrong though, and this was only natural reticence. Gurkhas, I'd noticed, are much more ready to socialise on equal terms with their military superiors than are the British.

Once I introduced a twenty-three year old Gurkha to Viscount Slim, son of the wartime general, Bill Slim. Our boy was completely unfazed. Sure, Lord Slim had been a Gurkha officer and had commanded the SAS, but he was, just like our lad, someone who'd served the Queen with due honour, and shared the glory of a joint calling. Although respectful, Gurkhas have enormous self-possession and dignity. 'I am a good man,' they seem to say 'and so are you.' Their phrase *Ma chhasto kholi chhiane*, there is no one like me, does not have the chest-beating self assertion of the Scottish 'Wha's like us?' but contains a quieter and literal truth. I am unique and uniquely special.

The previous year I'd been walking up to Edinburgh Castle with Corporal Kali who spotted a British officer in the give-away rifle green blazer and RGR tie. That this was Colonel David Hayes, Colonel of the Brigade, didn't inhibit him one bit. He was across the road in seconds, greeting the man in Gurkhali like an old friend. It has to be said that Colonel Hayes seemed overjoyed too. Clearly, there are different and happier inter-rank relations with this lot.

My flat was once turned into an impromptu Gurkha B&B when three pipers appeared at my door one Saturday evening on the sole basis that I had a spare room or two and was considered a friend. Some warning might have been in order but you couldn't help but be delighted. One was at the Army School of Bagpipe Music in Edinburgh and, he told me, was going to take a week's fishing holiday as the house guest of his brigadier, near Dingwall. As I said, a different breed.

As we stood outside waiting for a cab, an anxious neighbour asked if we were 'the plumbers.' 'No,' answered our boys, 'we're pipers.'

'What's the difference?' asked the lady.

'Quite a lot,' replied one.

Today, though, we were to rattle round Loch Ossian, hammer up the long roadless glen to the Ben Alder massif, trot through the pass which would take us to the treeless misnomer of Ben Alder Forest and finish at Dalwhinnie in time for tea. Moving twenty miles or so, north west, it would be an important leg in our trek which would take us right into the heart of Scotland

Past Loch Ossian we encountered a locked gate and wire fence, both well over twelve feet high. A staircase cum stepladder rose to its left permitting us access. There had been no deer behind us; somebody, somewhere wanted *their* deer kept on *their* side.

The map showed 'Corrour Shooting Lodge' and after a quiet hour's trek it emerged from the trees as a building site where the same someone was blowing a hell of a lot of cash. The neo-Victorian lodges and surrounding 48,000 acres are the property of Lisbet Rausing, eldest daughter of Hans Rausing, Britain's then richest man. On the northern edge of Loch Ossian was being built her £20 million home. *The Sunday Times* described it as 'the most sophisticated in the world'. Strange to say, that in a country strong on granite, Lisbet had imported 600 tons of the stuff from Portugal. Let's face it, when added to the plumbers' bill, you'd quickly run up £20 million.

Chez Lisbet is a glass-roofed castle, flanked by great towers pierced with conical windows, and employed over twenty Swedish interior designers all at the same time to get it right. As we entered this

Overleaf. *Left:* **Miles from nowhere – a typical coffee stop.**
Right: **Dhal models latest fashion accessory – antlers strapped to one's back. The deer in spotlight look.**

unexpectedly big complex, Dil whispered: 'Look. Deer.' He pointed dramatically as an elderly stag lumbered between the pines away from us. Then there was a second. It became obvious: they were all over the place and Kodak was about to make a killing.

'We can buy antlers here?' asked Dhal.

'Not sure,' I replied, knowing that we could lose a lot of time if we attempted to go shopping.

Although there were rows of shiny Range Rovers, and every lodge was in the middle of a major masonry transplant, we saw only one person, a rather smooth chap in tweeds stepping into a long-base Land Rover who gave us a quizzical but not unfriendly once over.

'There!' said Dhal triumphantly. Ahead was a low stone house with a heap of antlers piled on one side. I groaned inwardly.

'They can't *all* belong to someone?' asked Gyan hopefully, larceny rising.

Dhal was knocking on the front door while we all peered through a window to see a switched-on TV set, but no one within. Then three men with ruddy faces came out as one – which was a bit odd.

'Can we buy these?' asked Dhal.

There was a pause before it was established that the antlers were the property of Jack.

'Is Jack here?'

'I'm Jack,' replied a neat saturnine figure, tonelessly, hands in pockets. Jack had clearly never had the time to develop his social skills, and hadn't yet got round to eye contact. Instead, he sniffed the air like an animal, checking on its direction and strength, eyes on the hills above. His plus fours were caked in layers of old and new blood in an apron of grey and crimson. This was a proper ghillie.

'Are these for sale?'

'Tenner for that, twenty for those,' he indicated a good and then perfect set. 'Who are you?' he added truculently.

'We're walking through to Dalwhinnie,' said Ewen, 'to Stonehaven.'

Opposite: **Ewen taking in the cold headwind at Ben Alder. Loch Ossian is in the distance.**

Overleaf. *Left:* **Dhal looking like a Himalayan postman. Check out the thickly veined legs.**

Right: **Still time for tomfoolery as Dhal leads the way. Loch Ossian on the far horizon.**

Jack looked as mystified as if we had said Vladivostock. 'There's a few Munros here … '

'We're not climbing Munros. We started at Mallaig and we're heading for the North Sea,' I added,'

'Keep to the paths.'

'Oh yes,' I said, slowly aware of his concern.

'The other day I had a gun lined up for a kill when a bunch of hillwalkers came over the horizon and scared away all the deer.'

We shook our heads in sympathy, chuckling in sad disbelief. I think Surendra tutted. Don't overdo it, boys, he may think you're taking the piss. However, our credentials as fellow hillmen rather than bumbling anoraks established, his demeanour relaxed. This Jack was entirely centred on killing stags on this estate, and this estate only – and he was probably brilliant at it. Our boys were from the high Himalayas and they only wanted antlers; this computation took several minutes, but we got the antlers.

There's a curious tailpiece. Ewen was shooting pheasant in Fife a few months later and described his Corrour Lodge encounter. 'Jack?' exclaimed one of the guns. 'Oh yes, a maniac. We heard that Gurkhas had been through. About a week after your visit he drove a brand new Land Rover off a cliff trying to commit suicide.'

'Suicide? Good grief! What did you do?'

'Well, from now on he only gets to drive an *old* Land Rover.'

Only Gyan and Dhal eventually bought antlers. Dhal strapped his to his *jhola*, his pack, while Gyan ordered Surendra to carry his. Eventually, I boxed Gyan's antlers (you will not believe how big a box was needed) and sent it to his Dorset home and Ewen's company unwittingly paid for the delivery.

In the small strip between Loch Ossian's east end and the lodges were a small number of ponies and stags. But what's this? Black swans too!

'They're from Australia!' explained Ewen, describing why both he and his brother were surprised to see them. The loch has been designated an area of special protection because of its population of rare black-throated divers.

'And these are not black-throats?' asked Dhal, disingenuously.

Time to go. This was a straightforward plod eastwards up a glen that seemed featureless. Huge heather-clad mountains rose on both sides as we strode towards a distant cleft in the horizon along a peaty path. Typically, we were totally alone beneath a big sky, whose clouds were slowly lifting.

It would be impossible to get lost on a route like today's but half way up the glen we stopped to check the GPS to ascertain how many miles had been completed. The land was rising gently but there was little to judge our progress.

'We're here!' I poked the map. The boys crowded round. Good progress, and the burn we had followed, the Uisge Labhair, was now diminishing into an unholy peat hag.

'See up there, Neil?' indicated Dil with his chin, 'Deer.'

He was right. The long ridge high above us, the Aonach Beag, the Small Ridge, was dotted with little brown spots which were slowly keeping up with us.

I raised my binos. A flash came from a hollow to their rear. 'There's somebody up there,' I said.

'How many?' Oh great, they want a full intelligence report too.

'I'm not sure that there is anyone at all, I just saw something.'

Despite several sweeps by all the group, we couldn't spot the source of my flash, which I was certain was sun on metal.

Dil took the map and at high speed started naming every feature in sight: distant peaks, nearby crags and corries. I was impressed but bewildered. How could anyone interpret so quickly and with such certainty? 'See that, Neil, it's three-and-half kilometres away, isn't it?' I nodded dumbly but he gave me that look: the one worn by teenagers when explaining a computer sequence which is 'just *so* obvious'.

The end of the glen beckoned, with the Ben Alder massif towering on our right. The pass was our only way out of here and getting to it entailed marching up to a track high on the Ben's side.

The climb was a bugger. We split up into our own routes, tramping up the hillside with bursting lungs over the heather and juniper, anxious to reach the path as soon as possible. Ewen, ever fit and ever ready to take the lead, hit the track first and when we joined him, with only a mile to the pass, there was a universal agreement to flop down for lunch.

'That was hell,' I gasped, wiping sweat from my nose. The others (except Ewen) agreed, gulping air and reaching for drinks. Ewen, it must be said, did this all the time and was always way out in front instead of, fraternally, looking after his big brother. A show off, obviously, but a fit show off.

'Ben Alder? What does that mean?' asked Gyan.

'Ben of the rock water,' I replied

'Sock water?'

'No, *rock*!'

'Oh, maybe when it's wet, eh? Wet socks?' laboured Dhal, sucking on his Lucazade.

'Wasn't this where Cluny MacPherson had his famous cage?' I asked Ewen, referring not to an enclosure but a hideout.

'Yeah, Bonnie stayed a few days here before leaving for his French cruise. Cameron of Lochiel was here too.' Ewen is currently helping redesign the Culloden Visitors' Centre and knows his stuff.

Post Culloden, Charles Edward had moved from Knoydart to Ben Alder, where his diehard followers, Cameron of Lochiel and Cluny MacPherson, were resting in a long lost hideout. A description of Charles at the time says: 'He was bare-footed, had an old black kilt coat on, a plaid, philabeg [small kilt] and waistcoat, a dirty shirt and a long red beard, a gun in his hand, a pistol and dirk by his side.' The image of Tearlach behind a red beard was compelling, but the prospect of walking from Knoydart in bare feet was shocking. A few years before, I had met the author John Prebble in London who, although no great fan of the prince, considered his physical feats extraordinary, especially given the low calorie diet. 'Men today couldn't possibly survive, never mind thrive, in those conditions, like he did, for five months.'

The wind had grown like it always does in a pass, a natural funnel, and, as usual, it was in our faces. Although the path was dry, it rose sharply, and it was a struggle to keep up with my Nepalese friends who chugged up unthinkingly, like little quarry engines.

'This is like the Dolpa Pass in west Nepal,' shouted Gyan over the shrieking wind,

'To Mustang?' I yelled back.

'Yes. Twelve people died there last year.' Oh great. The Dolpa is the ancient trade route to Tibet, an ice cold lunar desert even in the summer.

Dil suddenly gripped my bicep: 'Look up there!' Three tiny human figures were disappearing over the skyline of the Aonach Beag on our left, following the deer herd. 'Tiny' doesn't really do justice; they were minute, barely discernable, specks.

'Of course,' I remembered, 'I'm with the best infantrymen in the world. They wouldn't miss a horizon-walker. To this day I'm not sure that I saw the flash I'd described earlier but somehow the three men on the Aonach confirmed to the Gurkhas that I possessed the type of qualities they admire. I was vindicated. Obviously, I hinted that I had been certain all along, but undeniable was that Dil's powers of observation were phenomenal.

At the throat of the pass was an untidy mess of plane parts.

'How long ago?' asked Gyan, seriously, surveying the aluminium bits and pieces.

'Long ago,' was my equally serious diagnosis. As leader I was called upon to opine on almost everything but forgotten plane crashes were above me. I had no idea what we were looking at and, for once, was going to keep quiet. Naturally, my will power evaporated after two minutes, and we were soon all agreeing that the aircraft must have tried to fly up the glen but crashed through bad weather or poor judgement, attempting to fly through the pass. The wind, even today in mid-summer, was ferocious and in a winter storm would represent destruction to an unaware pilot.

One of the many who had written pre-trek good luck messages was journalist Alasdair Roberts who told me of a Frenchman who, dressed up as a poncho-clad Clint Eastwood, had blown his brains out hereabouts with an old-fashioned Peacemaker. It had taken years to identify the body but Alasdair had come up here with the parents and played a lament on his pipes. It was a story too strange to share today.

Having attempted to prise free small 'souvenirs' from the plane, and failed, we moved off and found ourselves descending into a deep, plunging valley with only stone walls and slopes of gravel high above, with captured pockets of snow in the north-facing corries. The towering acres of grey spoil somehow reminded me of deserted American steel mills. Ahead of us, though, the landscape flattened into a promising green plain with low hills in the far distance.

The inevitable burn, the Allt a' Bhealaich Dhuibh, was joined by the Allt a' Bhealaich Bheithe, which led us through this grassless waste to a deserted lodge set on the plain below. Silent, long-maned ponies stood idle, their haunches into the wind, like wind-blown equine statues, seemingly lost in thought.

'Could we take those?' asked Dil. Here we go again, I thought, having previously explained the Theft Act as related to wildfowl and antlers. Now was the time to remind them that livestock fell within the legislation's embrace too.

'Just ride them for a couple of miles and set them free,' Gyan seemed hopeful.

'First, catch!' put in Surendra like some wise elder, short on words, long on perception.

'Nice idea though,' said Dhal.

Another four miles saw us cross the heath, the path over thick dry peat as comfortable as a sumptuous carpet. The area was alive with silent skylarks flitting from tussock to tussock. The wind, so malicious earlier that we'd sheltered in a shooting butt for coffee, had now dropped to a whisper so that the small Loch Pattack on our left looked as calm as a lake in the Home Counties.

The path hit a track which curved south, rightwards and down to Loch Ericht through wide-spaced pine. We crossed a cattle grid between eight foot high metal railings that were brand new and it occurred to us that everything we'd come across in the past five miles had been in perfect order. The drainage stones were smartly cut, paths neatly edged and even the occasional bridge seemed recently pointed. Yup, someone hereabouts had a ton of money.

'Take a look at this!' howled Ewen.

On the lochside road stood a fabulous turreted house, marked as 'Ben Alder Lodge'.

'Disney meets Carnegie!'

Everything about it was immaculate: clean stone, no moss, gleaming slates and not so much as a daisy out of place. It seemed brand new, finished yesterday. Pepper-pot turrets poked from towers on what was no more than a large house.

'Mind you, Carnegie was inventing, even then,' added Ewen, as if this new Highland folly could be forgiven on the basis of precedent.

Gyan seemed unmoved. 'This is a rich country. It's only right that money is spent on houses and paths. You can afford it.' I liked the 'you'.

Even the lochside road was in fabulous condition. Every bridge and culvert were so pristine they appeared alien. A small outcrop was fenced in dressed limestone so that a single tree and some garden furniture could take up a stately position as if it were overlooking, not Loch Ericht, but Monaco harbour.

'We'll be in Dalwhinnie in an hour if we keep up a steady pace, arriving at five,' I announced, suddenly realising the folly of asking Gurkhas for a 'steady pace' over tarmac. Surendra and I fell into step. 'Tell me about how you learned English.'

There was a long pause before he slowly began. 'I learned at school. In my last year we had a book that we had to learn.'

'What book?'

'Mr Charles Dickens, *Hard Times*.'

'Good grief, I read that at school too and it was 'hard times'!'

His lips flickered in a quick smile: 'I was not good at English.'

'But now?'

'We had lessons. I was intake 2000 and it was not easy.'

I recalled a story of this induction period where recruits were asked to write about a visit to a nearby town. 'Every person is very rich,' wrote one, 'Even the beggars wear pearls.' It transpired he'd described a lady collecting for the lifeboats.

My Nepali is pretty terrible and the conversation continued like this for half an hour. Surendra had just passed the airborne selection course, quite easily, I gathered, which I imagine, is a fair bit tougher in the Brigade of Gurkhas than in the regular British Army. Real deep waters here. It took me about five minutes to establish that the blue pheasant is Nepal's national bird. But it passed time and allowed me to forget my knees were apparently undergoing their shock absorber trials, tarmac section.

A tight dark forest rose on our left, its shadows a death sentence to all flora below where lay only a suffocating bed of needles. On the right lay twelve miles of Loch Ericht, one of the great brooding volumes of water

Overleaf. *Left:* **Looking back at Aonach Beag where deer could be seen near the summit.**
Right: **Ben Alder Lodge. Disney meets Carnegie. Check out Ewen's boots!**
Next page. **Loch Ericht. Two hardy breeds. Surendra and Dil take a breather on the road to Dalwhinnie.**

in the Highlands. Only a mile across, it seemed mysterious and powerful beneath its immense surface. What lay in its black depths?

At last came the end of the loch, and with it a magnificent gatehouse complete with the world's biggest cattle grid. I think it was made for a 747. Not just coaches, we were led to believe, passed through this extraordinary entrance. All this time, we never saw anyone, even though newly minted Land Rovers were lined up alongside the occasional cottage. Highland cattle lumbered between the road and shore as if this were Michael Jackson's Neverland 'ranch' moved to Scotland. Only llamas and Bubbles were missing. Someone had built themselves a real Highland fantasy out here. I'm sure that a shortbread tree would have been admired and accepted as utterly genuine too.

Ewen and Dil had arrived before me at Dalwhinnie and Gyan and Dhal were five minutes behind. Not only Campbell and his mercy-mission van awaited but a dozen-strong crowd of well-wishers too who were busting to greet us.

This was one of the many occasions when I was not at my best. It took me minutes to digest that I actually knew one couple (embarrassingly, Edinburgh neighbours) but Gyan was on top form as a PR natural and chatted happily to everyone. One was a former Royal Navy Commander who presented me with a postcard of his old ship, *HMS Gurkha*, and another was a retired Gurkha officer who had been instrumental in implementing the Brigade's English language policy. We were stunned to hear that some had 'come up the road from Pitlochry' which made us realise just how far we had walked.

On the hills it was normal not to have a mobile phone signal but now we were back in civilization, albeit only Dalwhinnie. I called *The Scotsman* Diary in Edinburgh to file some copy, trying to chivvy up the brain cells to spout something snappily journalistic. There was plenty to say, but where to begin? There was Dil's wonderful Newcastle-Edinburgh muddle, ScotRail's free ticket rescue, oh, and the weather. The Diarist, Simon Pia, had a good laugh but seemed reluctant to believe Dil's cock-up. However it appeared in the next day's paper under the heading 'Tyne Out'. *The Scotsman*, and Simon Pia in particular, are good friends of the Gurkhas and their readers have a long record of lavish donations. The crowd at Dalwhinnie pushed cash and cheques on us too. When this is all over, I thought, I'm going to miss complete strangers giving me cash.

It took an hour to drive back to Spean Bridge, meaning that if we were to start walking at 8 a.m. the next day, we had to leave at 7 a.m. Working backwards, we ought to have breakfast at 6.30. Alex Ferguson couldn't have been more helpful; it would be whatever we wished. As a former hotel breakfast waiter, I winced on behalf of his staff, but our Longest Day loomed and we had no option.

Gyan and I retired to our room early, but first I checked Chandra's knee. He had both radio and TV blaring out at the same time as if making the most of the hotel's facilities. It was only a surprise that both shower and bath weren't running too.

V

The Longest Day: To Braemar

~~~

Today was such a big one, nearly forty miles from Dalwhinnie to Braemar, that I couldn't bring myself to explain just how big. Months before, I had stood looking at a blank map of Scotland and come to the slow realisation that if we were to go from Mallaig to Stonehaven there was no alternative. I couldn't mumble 'forty miles', even though I tried. Furthermore, the route, over the Cairngorm itself, was what we planners call 'challenging'. All the same, I'd been guilty of putting this potential nightmare on the back boiler.

This was the heart of Scotland, where the rivers, instead of flowing west, would run eastwards. We'd move from Highland Region to Grampian and say goodbye to Spean Bridge. It was, no matter how I dressed it up, a terribly long walk.

After a small map-reading squabble, we were crunching up a bulldozer track surfaced with loose apple-sized stones which were ideal for twisting ankles. High bare hills interlocked in the sky around us, mighty but not impregnable.

The boys were unfazed, though Dil had sat with the maps, chin in hand, for an unsettlingly long time, but looked up with a grin. 'Looks a good day,' he said warmly.

I could hardly apologise for Scotland's geography but felt gratified that everyone left the hotel looking forward to a proper day's trek. Alex Ferguson had been up to see us off and donate a substantial sum as well as leather bookmarks embossed with the Commando Memorial. Chandra, though, had hobbled to breakfast, and could not be with us.

'When I was a boy, I had to carry oil drums up the hill to my home village, two at a time, and the wire used to cut into my arms, was very sore,' said Dil, explaining why today's march to Braemar hadn't exactly worried him. Gurkhas always call the Himalayas, *pahard*, the hill.

'Oil drums?' I queried.

'Cooking oil, we have no electricity.'

'Oh, you mean those little vegetable oil drums!' I held my thumb and index finger an inch apart, grinning.

'They were very heavy for a small boy,' he replied with mock offence and dismissive wave. I bet they were, and this helped explain Dil's extraordinary musculature.

Dalwhinnie, perhaps the least-loved village in the Highlands, fell away behind us. Bonnie Prince Charlie had come through it in '45 but promptly moved south to Perth where, in the excited realisation that this was really happening, had proclaimed his father as king. Queen Victoria had spent a bitter night here in 1861 moaning how 'there was hardly anything to eat: two miserable starved Highland chickens, without potatoes! No pudding and no fun.' Imagine a hotel receiving such royal censure today! Can you see the headlines? It came as a shock when Ewen quietly confessed to having designed the visitors' centre for the Dalwhinnie Distillery. This is the only attractive part of the village – and, of course, I'm not just saying that.

Above, USAF Tomcats scoured the clouds as the team turned off the road and headed along sheep tracks through thick heather, whose roots were a dangerous series of tripwires. Heather moorland covers a quarter of Scotland's land surface but is contracting fast under pressure from forestry and sheep so that we have lost about 25% of our heather since the mid 1940s. Although nothing will compare to their blossoming in the late 1800s, there remain about three hundred private estates which shoot 250,000 grouse per year. Heather, the birds' principal food, is burned regularly in strips, allowing young plants to grow. It's a tough bush; where sheep remove up to 40% of the season's growth it will persist.

Rabbits sprinted from beneath our boots, but it took several hours marching before the heather subsided from the hip-brushing stuff to ankle height. I didn't know it, but from now on every rabbit was on warning.

'Tyaha! Tyaha!' There! There! yelled Dhal as a furry shape darted away, with our sergeant in full Gurkha charge, yards behind. There were whoops of laughter as Surendra and Dil joined in the chase. Ewen and I bawled encouragement as the trio spread out keeping the rabbit within a triangle. The wee thing tried its best to break out, switching and swerving as its route was cut off by an arm-waving soldier. After thirty seconds the rabbit keeled over in sheer fatigue and fear. Dil pounced, grabbing it by the scruff of the neck. Like the animal, I was astounded.

The chase had covered a hundred yards and we jogged over to inspect. A burst of further laughter rolled across the hillside; the rabbit, bleating like a lamb, had punched Dhal in the nose. I realised what the boys had done. By spreading out and forcing the animal to run to and fro they had quickly exhausted it, but the skill was in deploying swiftly and thinking as one. Like most animals whose only defence is flight, they don't have the stamina of predators, and are quickly caught. News to me, but today it was obvious.

'I have never seen anything like it! A rabbit, a bloody rabbit!' I raved. 'People'll never believe it! Let's get a picture of you.' The threesome posed like proud big game hunters, still laughing. Then Dil gave it a quick kiss and laid it on the ground. It promptly fell on its side but regained composure and within a minute hopped away, albeit in a chagrined lope, but what a tale to tell Mrs Rabbit!

Minutes later, they were at it again, but the new animal escaped and came running back up the hill towards me. I accelerated downhill into a flat-out gallop but caught my boot and found myself temporarily airborne before crashing head first into a spot of burnt heather stalks. My pack opened on impact, throwing the contents (water, camera, flask, lunch, binoculars) all over the place. The breath was knocked out of me. The boys howled and howled as if this had been my party piece, specially laid on. It wasn't clear sometimes whether I was providing the leadership or the entertainment. I couldn't stop laughing myself and the moment was to provide a sort of en route landmark, so that recalled events happened before or after Neil's fall. You will not believe, either, how burnt heather stalks can scratch thighs.

'You okay, Neil?' asked Dil, smiling.

'Yeah!'

Overleaf.   *Left:* **Captured alive! A Highland rabbit meets Dhal, Surendra and Dil. We let it go.**
Right: **Leaving Dalwhinnie behind us and tramping over dangerous apple-size rocks. No one twisted an ankle!**
Next page. **Another stop. Surendra takes a drink while I look ready to cry. Dil poses thoughtfully over the maps.**

'Sure your head didn't take a knock? Sure you can remember everything? Because you've left your stick up there,' he pointed with his thumb, Gurkha-style, up the hill.

The glen's shoulders lowered into long outstretched arms and the path took us blithely down its centre. Looking down at the dry peat beneath our boots, I said: 'Extraordinary stuff, peat. Less solids than milk. Some of our peat bogs are over 9,000 years old. Comfortable on the feet, too, like this.' Dhal and Gyan kicked it happily, sending the kind of sprays that gardeners would die for.

Peat is the classic acidic soil, and it smothers Scotland's upland areas. Not only is there little decomposition but it actually rises at a rate of something like 2 mm per annum, growing out of the protracted life of the dead. Human bodies, several thousand years old, have been discovered in peat bogs, so fresh-looking that police have been called, not archaeologists. The bodies inevitably get the nickname 'Pete' or 'Doug'.

Our rock types have had clear effects on soil formation. It's an extraordinary fact, but the country has almost no calcium at all. This is why our water is soft and soil acidic. Calcium is the key nutrient harnessed by plants and its absence has severe implications. The word 'acidic' is used carelessly; soil acidity is measured on the pH (potential of Hydrogen) scale, meaning that soils below a pH of 4.5 are acidic, whereas those of above have a neutral or high pH. Without calcium acting as an alkali and without the protection of trees the land becomes quickly saturated and, together with acidic soils we are left with conditions that are ideal for blanket bog. Altitude too has an important effect on growth (check out our Gurkha friends), and the higher you go, the lower the height of the heather, juniper and bilberry grass.

These ruminations had a severe downside. It soon became clear that there was something wrong with the landscape. Not that it was polluted or built over, only that it was missing a loch. A rather vital loch. This was bad news indeed. We'd slept-walked down the glen far too far and now realised we had strolled off the map altogether. My pride was stung, and we practically stamped the two miles over to where we should have been. You always know when you're on the wrong path; the pieces don't quite fit, but you kid yourself until the obvious becomes undeniable. Walking along the edge of a map is dangerous too, because you don't know what should be on the other side. Today, though, we just hadn't paid attention.

We found a picnic spot on a weir but the wind grew, made vindictive by slivers of rain, but comfort was had. When the weather turns, hot drinks have a disproportionately cheering effect and today the coffee was magnificent. Dil and Surendra quickly built a fire too, and the bright flames gave an unexpected welcome warmth.

Three miles of thick sodden heather took us to the foot of a dramatic climb which rose a thousand feet into the sky. We had to climb it and then swing right along the skyline.

'Is that a convex or concave slope?' I asked Dhal mischievously. He gave me the 'C'mon, kid. I'm-a-Gurkha-sergeant' look and said nothing.

'Convex,' replied Surendra. 'You can't see top, so it's convex.'

Another bugger. A thick pine forest ran on our right, over the horizon, and I fell behind almost immediately as the boys trudged powerfully upwards. Someone seemed to be holding on to my pack, pulling me back. At the middle section the guys waited for me to catch up.

'Neil, we could go through this,' Gyan indicated a path through the forest. He was right, *if* the path went through the forest, it was a short cut. However, I knew from experience that paths in untended forest like this have a habit of suddenly disappearing, leaving the walker facing a wall of impenetrable brush.

There was another short terse argument with Gyan, made worse by my inability to explain the possibility that we'd get half way through and then have to come all the way back. This was a language thing but Gyan was unwilling to accept my decision without further debate.

I knew this wasn't a good line but used it anyway: 'Gyan, that's my decision. We keep going up this hill and turn right at the top. I know what I'm doing, please accept it!'

Needless to say, we stormed to the horizon and then laughed about it. This was another good moment: we were now on to our fourth map. A wee ceremony might have been appropriate but it was a fillip all the same. The new route was a long bulldozer road which swept east through thick heather where grouse called loudly. Three valleys met way below us and we descended at a rapid march, covering the five miles of switchback track to Glen Feshie as if going in to attack the place.

The long slope down was in full summer purple, while the deep green forestry set it off like the Wimbledon colours. The sun burst through as if announcing glory days ahead. Glen Feshie was a long, mostly grass-covered valley with a handful of wondrous oaks, while one side was hemmed in with a long grey cliff, trimmed with pines as if this were Montana. All it needed was for a couple of clapboard houses and we could have filmed a Western here.

Because of the grass, it looked lived in but was quite empty, though we were far from being its first visitors. Guess who had been here before us? Queen Victoria and Prince Albert on one of their rundfahrts had ridden through on ponies all the way from Balmoral, complete with kilted, hamper-laden attendants in September 1860. The royal couple, going under the curious travel names of Lord and Lady Churchill, visited a cottage here which had been Edward Landseer's 'encampment' and admired the frescos of stags above the fireplace, ate a picnic by the river, then pushed north. They returned in October 1861 but Albert was dead within three months and the 'Royal Glen Feshie' period died with him. Only the cottage's lum still remains, but there is precious little today that hints at the area's celeb-filled past.

There was a moment of deep concern as we sat round frowning at the maps. There were twenty-five kilometres/sixteen miles to go and it was nearly five o'clock. Just how late was our finish going to be? Perhaps 10 p.m. There was a taxing march out of the glen, keeping on until we reached the watershed, then a long hike down to Braemar, crossing almost an entire OS map, and no way of contacting Campbell. The prospect was not so much daunting as beyond comprehension. Even the question, 'How did I get into this?' seemed unanswerable.

'Let's cross the glen first,' said Ewen, and lumbered off across the grassy floodplain with the rest trailing. The River Feshie was broad and low, and it was nearly possible to keep one's boots dry by crossing on the big granite boulders. Nearly, but not quite. We stopped to wring out our socks and grab a snack in a spot where I imagined Albert and Victoria had picnicked. Gurkhas have been serving the British Crown since 1815, when Farmer George had been on the throne. Victoria knew all about the Gurkhas, and was probably the first monarch who did. The ruler of Nepal, Maharajah Jungbahadur Rana, had visited Britain and pledged his faith to the Queen during a Buckingham Palace audience, which, as a Gurkha himself, had not been given lightly. Together the 'British' Gurkhas and 10,000 of the Nepalese Army helped save the Raj during the Mutiny. From 1857 onwards British soldiers began speaking of 'Them Gurkees of ours' and ever since they have been welcome in all messes. The Gurkhas themselves always preferred to pitch their lines near the British and not beside the *madhise*, plainspeople. In 1863 Queen Vic presented the 2nd Gurkha Rifles with a famous Truncheon, an ornamental man-size staff complete with little kukris and Gurkha figures holding her crown atop, to commemorate their service in the Mutiny. The Truncheon replaced the colours no longer carried as the Gurkhas became rifle regiments in recognition of their achievements. Without ever being part of the British Empire, Nepal has provided us with more continuous support than any other of our so-called allies. I wondered how many of the Gurkhas had taken the Queen/Empress's rupee in the expectation that they would one day follow in her actual footsteps.

'This is very beautiful,' said Gyan, 'Why don't people farm here? It looks good. There should be a village here.'

'My home village could move here' said Dil wistfully.

'How big is your home village?' asked Ewen.

Dil puffed out his cheeks and waved his hands expansively: 'Oh, hundreds of people!'

We rested under the big Scots pines, aware that the day was far from over but happy and confident. The glen's sunlit tranquillity added to our sense of ease. We were witness to this because we had walked here – and we'll walk out again. Ever wondered why there are no pictures of Glen Feshie on calendars of Bonnie Caledonia? Because some photographer would have to walk twenty miles in and twenty miles out: that's why. There is a huge square in the very heart of the Scottish Highlands that almost never appears in print *anywhere*.

There was a touch of contentment in the air. Feshie babbled its way north to join the Spey and we had again found ourselves in a lost paradise. We were united and ready for the last leg of today's marathon in a manner that would have impressed any of those daft motivation coaches. *'Tayah, ketaharu?* Ready, lads?' I asked, as they leapt to their feet. It was important that we (especially me) strolled rather than ran the next fifteen miles, but I felt bitter regret that when we found a world-class beauty spot, we couldn't spend an hour or so pottering.

The initial route took us along a scary track along the scree slope above the river where occasional landslips made it downright dangerous. At one point it reduced to a steep hillside of gravel, so that a stumble would lead to a rapid and painful descent. But we cleared it and continued up the glen which narrowed into a gorge, and the river grew increasingly energetic with a run of fabulous waterfalls. It was not the time for conversation and the pace became correspondingly manic.

After a couple of hours we had broken the back of it and were on the tussocked uplands where the horizon was low and marked by gentle gradients. We crossed the River Eidart where I knew Victoria had crossed (and dropped a bundle of cloaks in the water) but a mile afterwards I noticed that to our south was a traditional Scottish peat bog set in a small depression. A hazard for others perhaps, but for us a point of some significance. From its eastern side snaked a trickle of black water, the Geldie Burn, and it flowed eastwards to the North Sea!

'Look, guys!' I pointed to both map and bog. 'We've not just hit the first river bound for the North Sea, we've just crossed the border from Highland Region into Grampian.' As the men had never heard of either Region, it meant disappointingly little.

'Are we in the Cairngorms?' asked Gyan.

'I'm not sure. Nearly. The Cairngorm National Park is just to the north of us. Look.' Again I fingered the map. Sure enough, the Park was about five miles away. The whole Cairngorm plateau is one massive granite intrusion, with Beinn MacDuibh as Scotland's second highest peak. It was only in the 1840s that the OS discovered that it was lower than Ben Nevis. Of course, loyal locals refused to believe this piece of nonsense. While Beinn MacDuibh is home to the *famh*, yes, a ferocious dog-sized mole, it is also the abode of the Grey Man, a giant figure who is explained as the spirit of the mountain or an ape-like member of the yeti race, *fear mhòr*. Another Scotland-Nepal link?

But the trek to Braemar was far from over; nine miles remained and the first four were of extraordinary boredom, tramping down an unending featureless sheep track where, again, we found ourselves hammering

Overleaf. *Left:* **Crossing Glen Feshie flood plain with Surendra dawdling. We had come down the pass in the background.**
Right: **In Grampian at last and six miles to Braemar We've hit the Land Rover track and have just over two hours to go.**
Next two pages. *Left:* **Marching down into Glen Feshie so determindedly you'd think we were going to attack the place.**
Right: **Dil looks askance at the empty Glen Feshie wondering where the village is.**

along, united in the urge to finish and to hell with any absorbing views. We didn't stop, and slowly, slowly the low-lying landscape pulled past. The path became a Land Rover track but this did not mean that Campbell could pick us up, as he and the vehicle were locked out of the estate, behind a gate at Braemar's Linn of Dee. Mobile phones didn't work anyway and we couldn't have called anyone for help, never mind our own transport.

We were all becoming utterly worn down with eleven hours of unrelenting walking. Spike Millligan once created a loony military historian who used to recreate the Battle of Waterloo in his bedroom using huge maps and vast numbers of pins to represent the troops. One night he force-marched a battalion of pins until their points were blunt. I was slowly understanding the description. I vaguely knew Spike in the late 1970s, enough for him to send a signed book on my father's 1982 retirement from the Army, with the dedication: 'This is the year that it's all going to happen!' Dad promptly became a student and his disintegrating dress sense became, temporarily, of family concern. That's how much my mind was wandering.

As we approached the Chest of Dee a hundred-strong herd of red deer, complete with young, stood their ground as we marched past. I suspect that had we stopped they'd have bounced away but none of us wanted to waste so much as a second taking in the view; snacks and drinks were taken on the move. There was no option, my knees could not be relied on to stop and then re-start within the same hour. On the final run in the deer numbers became bewildering. Thousands of the beasts were grazing in the evening sun from the road's edge to the skyline as unperturbed as if we were invisible.

There are about 350,000 deer in Scotland, double the figure of thirty years ago, and this represents a population growth out of control. They are rapacious suppressors of woodland regeneration, and chew up seedlings and saplings before they can grow. We still know little about their ranging behaviour but one 19th century writer commented: 'The deer forests of Scotland contain not a single tree. The sheep are driven from, and the deer driven to, the naked hills and then it is called a deer forest. Not even timber-planting and real forest culture.' The author? One Karl Marx, *Das Kapital, Volume I*. Quite why Karl should have digressed into Scottish deer estates is unknown. Was it a mistranslation that began 'Deer Workers of the World, Unite'? I blame the British Museum's Reading Room and its tempting Reference Section.

Marxists will feel vindicated to learn that there were once four villages around the Chest of Dee which were cleared by the Duke of Fife for deer in the 1850s, and that his erstwhile property, Beinn MacDuibh, was later sold to the American millionaire, Kluge, whose wife wanted to be a neighbour of Queen Elizabeth II. A mile north of where Campbell now waited was once a village in Glen Lui which was cleared in 1726 when Lord Grange, brother of the forfeit Earl of Mar, wrote to his factor: 'Eject these people after their harvest is over ... the more men you have with you the less will be the opposition ... people may see that they will not be suffered for their illegal insolence.'

Minutes after crossing a bridge where the young River Dee joined us from the left and with only two miles to go, my reverie was interrupted when the clump clump of Surendra's boots came thumping up behind me. He grinned but wordlessly jogged past, heading for Ewen and Dil, leaving Gyan, Dhal and me in his wake. I had been lost in a world of my own, a mental escape, as a reaction to the repetitive, robotic pace. The realisation that we were nearly there, that in minutes the whole forty-mile bash would be triumphantly completed, lifted my boots with a new energy. But Surendra, are you human, or what?

'Hey, Neil, well done!' congratulated Campbell and Chandra. Ewen and Surendra were already in the vehicle but I waited for the others to come in, feeling seriously drained but exuberantly happy. The lads strolled in, chatting conversationally, looking up as if to say, 'Oh, here we are, the end of our walk.' What was to me a triumph was to them a mere accomplishment, taken on and fulfilled in the normal Gurkha way. It was 9.10 p.m. We'd been on the go for over thirteen hours, and they didn't seem particularly affected. From the watershed to the Linn of Dee is an unbroken descent of only 150 metres. We'd enjoyed a perfect golden evening too. Had the last ten miles been uphill or even undulating – and in filthy weather – how late would we have been?

'I've had real problems with supper, Neil,' said Campbell. Nobody in Braemar, it seemed, could provide us with anything to eat this late in the

Overleaf. *Left:* **The ubiquitous red deer, whose population had doubled in thirty years and is clearly out of control.**
Right: **Gurkha gourmets. Dil eats as Gyan directs the spare rib deployment. Campbell tucks in, oblivious.**

evening. 'The B&B though is great, I've put the luggage in the rooms. You've got one to yourself.' The van roared round to the Mayfield – a magnificent Highland house where the rooms had a real old-world stateliness about them that was peculiarly Scottish. Our landlady wrung her hands in apology that she hadn't got any supper for us and advised we check out the town immediately. 'Right, guys, showers when we come back – we're leaving now!'

'I think we ought to change out of our boots!' said Gyan intelligently.

'Okay, up to your rooms and change! But nothing else! We've got to hurry!'

'I'm putting on a different jacket,' replied Ewen.

'Well, okay, boots and jackets. Then back here, *cheeto*! Hurry!'

'My socks are wet,' put in Dhal.

'Now, you're just taking the Mickey! This is like the Spanish Inquisition sketch. Okay, okay, our changes *include* boots, jackets and socks.'

Minutes later, gathered outside the chip shop, we were appalled to discover it was closed. 'It's not even ten o'clock!'

'Some tourist town this. They make all their money in a few summer months. You'd think a chippie would be open until ten,' groaned Campbell. The town, it must be said, looked great, clean, with lots of grass, and full of wealthy visitors taking the evening air in bright cashmere jerseys. Italians, we reckoned.

'Does cashmere come from Kashmir?' asked Dil, confusingly – a query that works best as a written question – but I knew what he meant because I'd asked the same question myself in my mid-twenties.

We tried a grand hotel, the Fife Arms, but they'd stopped serving and recommended Ballater, the next village along the Dee. Everywhere we asked had just stopped serving, like a game someone was playing. By now darkness had fallen and the moon was out. The decision was made to go back to Braemar and simply have a pint.

We got the lager but the posh hotel we chose refused to serve us even crisps on the outrageous basis that we were non-residents. The barman blushed with embarrassment but it was the rules. 'Try this sort of service in New York,' I told him, 'and see the reaction. You have plenty of

American visitors here, don't you? What do they make of this kind of behaviour?'

I wasn't particularly rude nor even loud, I didn't have the energy. We drank our beer sitting in armchairs set in the foyer, in comfort, but so late we had gone beyond hunger. 'Only seven hours till breakfast,' announced Ewen with great glee. Gyan looked grim but no one complained. Back in our B&B we sat down and guzzled Mars Bars with coffee, before slipping into sleep, knowing that Ewen was right, and that a full Highland breakfast was even nearer. Perhaps we should have kept that rabbit.

VI

Dark Lochnagar

~~~

A wonderful smell of cooking wafted up the stairs and roused the lads like an irresistible olfactory alarm clock. From the corridor could be heard the gargling, hacking and trumpeting noises that Gurkhas make while washing as if a baby elephant were in with them. Though most are never quite sure what the bathmat is for, all Gurkhas wash vigorously and make the average British soldier look like something from the Black Lagoon. Outside the weather was grey but there was something subtle about the light that said 'Highlands'. We had been asked to close the garden gates when we returned the previous night to prevent deer entering the garden. Not a common instruction.

Any team that is walking over twenty miles a day will find it practically impossible to overeat at breakfast; we had walked forty and hadn't had a proper meal for twenty-four hours. The landlady must have reckoned we had bionic stomachs, or were feeding invisible dogs beneath the table. We ate well, very well. Strangely, we were no more hungry this morning than on any other but perhaps it was the air that was the special ingredient – the house had a warm aroma that spoke of comfort, home-made biscuits and blazing hearths. If you had a perfect Highland granny, she'd live here. Gyan was asked to sign the visitors' book, an act he was proud to fulfil.

'Do you want me to put my Dorset address?'

'No, no,' replied the landlady, 'The one in Nepal!'

Of course, I expect landladies hold an annual convention and boastfully display exotic addresses from their visitors' book like a group of Hyacinth Bouquets; a hill village near Everest has got to be worth a good crow, at least.

Braemar, though famous for its royal connections, has a mixed history. The 1715 Rebellion exploded when Bobbin' Jock, or Erskine, Earl of Mar, raised the Stuart standard here. The knob at the top fell off which everyone saw as a terrible omen. They were right, the rebellion ended almost immediately. A month after Culloden the Government troops swept into Deeside, burning houses, but as the main landowners, the Gordons and the Farquharsons, had supported the king, it couldn't have been too wild. Nota Bene: the landowners were not *all* the Gordons, nor *all* the Farquharsons. Rather, two individuals whose whim could bring disaster.

Queen Victoria bought Balmoral in 1852 for 30,000 guineas after the Royal Physician, Sir James Clark, had recommended the area on account of its famously 'dry climate' (curious figure: £30,000 was on Charlie's head). Then Lord Aberdeen, a future PM, had pushed the purchase of Balmoral, the property of his brother, Robert Gordon. Albert thought it looked like Thuringerwald and Switzerland. He redesigned the place, they entered it in 1855 and almost immediately the whole family went tartan mad with Scotland seen through the writings of Scott, the oils of Landseer and the fawning attentions of lairds and manly attendants. Her Majesty's affection, though, was genuine and it was her support for the Braemar Games that helped them survive and flourish.

As a piper who had played at the Queen Mum's hundredth birthday parade on Horse Guards Parade, Dhal knew all about royalty and the Games, and asked to be photographed by the Braemar road sign.

'Look at that!' he read, 'A tourism award-winning town!'

'Aye, right!' said Campbell.

'Except that we can't be bothered with tourists if it means we've got to work late during the summer,' added Ewen. Our team was still incredulous that food had not been available anywhere in Braemar before ten o'clock, but the town could still smugly proclaim its excellence.

I filed some copy for *The Scotsman* excoriating the place under the headline 'Highland Welcome?' which appeared the next day. The shut chippie was castigated and the posh hotel that was above serving crisps to non-residents after 9 p.m. was not forgotten. Later I wrote a thousand-

Overleaf. *Left:* **Dhal, a piper who had played at the Queen Mother's 100th birthday, knew all about Braemar and insisted on his picture while dismissive of the town's hospitality.**
Right: **Above Loch Callater. The weather closing in and time to zip up jackets.**

Next page. **Ascent into lowering cloud prior to a huge climb before the Lochnagar plateau. If Queen Victoria could do it, then so could we.**

word article which named every hotel that had done us down. Unfortunately, I'd forgotten that people actually read *The Scotsman* and a return visit in the company of Gurkhas is likely to be a little awkward for some time to come. There were letters and phone calls of complaint, my dears, along with one envelope, however, that contained the article with the offending lines circled and the inked words: 'Been there, done that!'

We found ourselves walking up Glen Callater, heading for Loch Muick over the Lochnagar plateau which rises to 1,000 metres (Ben Nevis peaks at only 1,344 metres). It was a long track with the usual rolling heather-clad hills to each side. Chandra was back with us, knee bandaged and hair magnificently quiffed. Dil had seriously assured me that Brylcreem was a hair restorative, while Surendra's coiffure was always plastered with the stuff. This was for when we were in the hills. Of course, when they got dressed up things got serious.

It was calm until we reached Loch Callater, when we swung left and began some steep climbing. In seconds a rabbit leapt from the heather and the lads, laughing loudly, belted after it, but it evaded them and ran across the path twelve yards from me. I grabbed my blackthorn by the sharp end and hurled it, ball handle first, at the sprinting animal. The knobkerrie head struck and sent the animal's body cartwheeling. Then it came to a dead stop. There was a huge roar from the boys. I'd killed it!

Ewen immediately reacted as if this were premeditated murder. 'There was no need to kill it, Neil. The guys just like to chase them. Remember yesterday?'

This show of piety prompted Chandra, the little swine, to concur: 'Is sad, no?'

'C'mon, I didn't mean to. It just ran across me and I threw my stick at it. I'm hardly the rabbit-murderer of old Lochnagar.'

Dhal and Dil though, bless, were full of admiration. 'Right on the head! Right on the head!' they enthused. I was indeed the mighty hunter, albeit without fraternal approval. Climbing further up the hill, it crossed my mind that the incident would bring bad luck, but then recalled the many myxy rabbits I've dispatched with the same stick. Announcing that

Overleaf. *Left:* **Surendra and Chandra contemplate a winter's day, 1st August, minutes from the peaked Lochnagar.**
Right: **Coming off Lochnagar. The small figures in the middle distance are Chandra, Surendra and Dil who have forgotten how slowly I move.**

I'd killed plenty before wasn't, I suspected, going to mitigate today. I cursed Ewen, though, for making me feel so guilty about a bloody rabbit.

Perhaps it was the morning freshness or that we were now much fitter after five full days of marching, but we were quickly high above the loch. 'Down there a raiding party of Campbells coming back from Glen Shee was ambushed in 1644,' I pointed to the loch's southern end, 'And somewhere around here there's a well that miraculously melted during a freezing winter, when no one had water.'

'Why didn't they just melt snow or ice in fire?' asked Chandra.

'Oh, there's always one, isn't there, who spoils the story? I describe a miracle and you come up with a smart-Alec question that ruins it!' I laughed. We stopped for a coffee with Surendra, Chandra and Dil sitting on a huge rock, like survivors on the upturned hull of a giant yacht. The valley leading away south from the loch looked as if it had been perfectly scooped by some Ice Age behemoth: the shape was geometric.

Grouse were everywhere and it was pretty obvious that they were with young that they didn't want to abandon. Consequently, mother bird would dawdle dangerously before a stone would zing past her beak, followed by another and another. The birds didn't seem to realise they were under attack. How Dil and Chandra didn't actually hit one practically defied the rules of probability. What was extraordinary was how a fat dozy bird would appear on the path well ahead of us and within a split second a salvo of pebbles had nearly taken her toes off.

Eventually, one of Surendra's spun into a bird's side, making a dull thumping noise, which knocked the grouse clean over like a skittle. At last, it realised what was going on and flew off calling like an indignant banshee.

Heavy rain started coming down, and the wind, of course, was full in our faces. The rain jackets were zipped up and waterproof covers were pulled over packs. Our boots swung left round the hill on a contour, with visibility closing into a low grey wall. This was where I made my last great balls-up of the whole trek. Moving on to our fifth map in the driving rain, I simply didn't check the route. We had come to a col and, without thinking, just kept walking along the path.

After twenty minutes of sodden marching, with cold wet faces and hands, it dawned on me that we'd missed our turning. We tramped back in low spirits to the col. Dil took the map and quickly realised what had happened.

'We go up there!' his arm pointing up a stone path that climbed the col's shoulder into the cloud so steeply it appeared more like a cliff. This led up to Carn an t-Sagairt Mòr, currently disguised as a Himalayan foothill. No wonder I'd missed it; we weren't supposed to be cresting hills, and my route radar hadn't registered this monstrous anomaly. A brief cup of coffee, though, revived my spirits. I blamed that blasted wabbit.

Gyan realised this wasn't the moment for reproach: 'Well, we've certainly got a climb here, eh? I'll go last.' Comfortingly, he didn't add: 'Behind Neil.' You're alright, Gyan, really.

My thighs felt as if they'd been wrapped in an ice compress, and I wasn't alone. 'You know, Neil, we ought to have more emergency clothes for days like this,' said Ewen in a serious voice. I chattered assent. This was the 1st August, for God's sake.

The climb was appalling. Steep steps rose into the mist like *A Matter of Life and Death*, where neither the top nor the bottom were visible. The lads tore off ahead leaving me forsaken and panting my lungs out. Because it was unexpected, I was not psychologically prepared; it was the equivalent of someone coming into your work and saying, 'You! Five mile run. Now!' I knew that if I really ran at this something inside would explode: perhaps my ears, perhaps my heart; something under pressure would suddenly go 'pop'. And I thought we had planned to avoid all seriously high climbs? Of course, I'd forgotten that the pass was nearly the height of Ben Nevis. Treachery, treachery.

Gyan stayed with me, plodding slowly in my footsteps, puffing, but with me. No, I wasn't going to pretend I was outrunning him, but at least I wasn't out of sight of everyone.

'C'mon Neil, it's freezing up here!' called Ewen. The rain had turned to snow and the poor darlings were getting cold waiting. Under rivulets of sweat, my sympathies were non-existent. However, his voice was reassuringly close and within a minute the group could be seen like ghosts looming out of the mist.

'Neil Saheb, *salaam bhanchha*!' greeted Dhal, as if he hadn't seen me for days.

'Welcome to Scotland!' I joked, taking a minute to recover, before we moved off along a contour just beneath the ridge before transforming into seven boot-clad icicles. There was almost no vegetation, just flat stones, now rapidly becoming covered in snow flakes. Ptarmigan ran off in a low crouch, their wings still handily winter-white. Christ, this was tundra, in August! I recalled that the Balmoral street party on Coronation Day, June 1953, was blown away by 'the Balmoral Blizzard'. That was the day the news of Everest's conquest was on the front pages. How bloody appropriate.

The route looped back so that without the mist we'd be looking down at Loch Callater again. Instead, in the thick mist we stumbled over a frozen corpse, that of a red deer hind.

'Had that been a stag, the antlers would have been gone in seconds,' commented Ewen. As he spoke, Chandra was turning the jaw, checking to see if there was anything worth removing.

We dipped into a grassy re-entrant where a burn spattered in a thin deep trench. Another snack break, where Surendra, despite the cold, removed his boots and washed his feet. Chandra chomped silently on a banana, while, I, yet again, wondered why mine always ended up as a bottom-of-the-pack mash.

'Remember when we were waiting for you at that narrow waterfall past Corrour Lodge?' asked Ewen. 'Surendra did an amazing thing. When we were looking over the waterfall, his hat fell off and he jumped after it, except he leapt from side to side down the gorge and grabbed his hat about two seconds after it hit the water! He bounced down off the walls like a circus act – and didn't even end up in the water!'

There are said to be 84,000 Buddhist teachings, one for each of the ways the human mind confuses itself. Today was like life itself: pushing onwards, taking guidance from the clues around us, while being aware that there was a bigger picture beyond the fog. The philosophy served us well. Aware of dim crags on our left we headed for the summit of Lochnagar in a rising, perishing wind without anyone pointing out that it had never been part of our schedule. We were going to ascend one of the country's great peaks accidentally.

The boys had assumed Lochnagar was, quite understandably, a loch. But it has eleven peaks, all over 3,000 feet, and is best remembered by a haunting pipe tune and Byron's lines, 'The deep frowning glories of dark Lochnagar'. Queen Victoria, of course, had been here before us, spending twenty minutes shivering on its summit in 1848, but it had defeated

Gladstone, while Disraeli stayed at Balmoral, always coming over faint in the Highland outdoors, which he described as 600 miles from civilization. Queen Vic managed to bag a total of eight Munros in her lifetime, including Beinn MacDuibh, Beinn a' Bhùird and the first *recorded* ascent of Carn a' Chlamain, which put her then in an elite group of only a dozen people – mostly scientists, cartographers and cranks.

For the first time in our trek, we came across fellow walkers and didn't know whether to be happy or displeased. Were they an intrusion or company? In thirty years there has been a ten fold increase in the number of hillwalkers in Scotland. The tops of Ben Nevis and Cairngorm can have a thousand visitors a day, while 60,000 ascend Ben Lomond annually. The erosion brought on by this onslaught has never been quantified, though mountain bikers are felt to be an even bigger cause of hillside damage. In 2003, 200,000 mountain bikers visited trails around Scotland, as compared with 150,000 skiers. It's pretty obvious that something's got to give at some locations, soon, and that our Twelve Passes route had ensured we were the lucky ones. We'd always had the hills to ourselves and now some dreadful busybodies were crowding us. There must have been, oh, ten of the buggers. In fact, you more or less have to smile at each other; it's the law. Two, it transpired, were from the RAF Mountain Rescue on their day off and were delighted to shake hands.

Our ascent to the trig point felt like a group of Hobbits advancing to an unexpected but deserved triumph. How strange! We couldn't see anything. On a clear day we could have spotted Ben Nevis in the west and the Pentland Hills south of Edinburgh, eighty miles away. The lads had wanted to have Balmoral pointed out to them but it is blocked by hills anyway. Instead we were being blown apart in a dense icy mist.

'You know, until recently, if you phoned the Royal Family at Balmoral, a servant used to answer 'Ballater 213', even though they got all digit numbers years ago,' I said.

Gyan chuckled at this *lèse-majesté*. Gurkhas come from a kingdom and are happy with monarchy. So much so that Queen Elizabeth is called *Hamro Maharani*, Our Queen.

A few months later I took two Gurkhas who were stationed in Edinburgh for a pint in a flash New Town bar and had mentioned that Prince William was known to frequent the place. When we met up again, it transpired that the twosome had spent almost every free hour since then sitting in the same pub hoping to meet the prince.

We stood on the concrete pinnacle and spotted two white songbirds fluttering in coy flirtation. 'They're snow bunting,' explained a couple clad in Arctic gear. Snow bunting! I was transfixed. How many climb Lochnagar and see snow bunting? I was thrilled. The other walkers must have looked at our lot, clad in shorts, cavorting on the gravel, and wondered if we knew anything about hillwalking at all.

This elevated state lasted twenty minutes; any longer and one of us would have fallen victim to hypothermia, but our descent route was unclear. The whole massif comprises two huge U-shaped crags, each centred with a wee loch, Lochnagar and Loch nan Eun (Loch of the Birds). We had strolled in from the west and wanted to go south, but it took a compass bearing to take us in the right direction after Dil had recognised a patch of snow and realised we were retracing our steps. There were dangerous drops of several hundred feet which lurked at the edge of the path, like mantraps hidden in smoky mist. I suddenly became very concerned.

'Listen, guys, keep together. We must not split up. This whole area is very dangerous, so concentrate. Dil will lead.' The fear was genuine. Too many people die in the Scottish Highlands and I did not want to have to phone the MoD and tell them that I'd lost one of their Gurkhas. This was not fat boy from Edinburgh telling mountain lads how to tackle mountains, but an attempt to keep the group together. I didn't want any solo descents today.

The route was clearly marked by a run of small cairns, but even so Surendra and Chandra were dawdling. 'C'mon, guys, if we split up it'll take hours to find each other.' This was the only moment of the whole walk when I was genuinely anxious about safety, and I couldn't help but take it seriously.

In minutes we'd descended to below the mist line and escaped the cold wind. In fact, the temperature rose at a disproportionate rate. Normally, temperature increases by one degree Celsius for every 150 metres descended, but we had come from bad weather into sun, from bitter wind into stillness, and it was suddenly a gorgeous summer's day. However, Dil and the boys had taken it upon themselves to ignore the huge hairpin in the path and were leaping like amphetamine-fuelled airborne goats in a direct route to Glen Muick far below. This spelled trouble for me, as I am not built to fly between large blocks of granite and began timidly scrambling over and down stones the size of small houses, all the while hoarsely yelling at the guys to slow down. Ewen and Gyan were way on the right, having taken the hairpin path like the intelligent chaps they were. Chandra glanced back once but seemed convinced I was in no trouble; either that or the little devil was leaving me to it.

By the time I caught up the sun was full out, and our boots were throwing up orange dust. Coming round a corner we found a small group of stags only yards away, sitting in the sun, chewing the cud. It made good sense to join them and have a sandwich or two. They eyed us nervously but soon relaxed. It was an extraordinary moment; these were wild deer which normally leap away when within a hundred yards of man.

'I think that the alpha male, that big one there,' nodded Ewen, 'can't be bothered to move. So long as we keep our voices low, we shouldn't disturb them.'

Chandra and Surendra, having scoffed their food without a thought about sudden hand movement, now slowly and surreptitiously brought cameras up to their eye as if the stags might object. We had split the herd, so that the smaller group gingerly stepped across to join the others, their coats as glossy and glorious as racehorses. It couldn't last. Dhal started crawling towards the nearest animal which promptly got to its feet, as if offended, and the others followed suit. They moved only a few yards away, though, as if more in sadness than in anger.

It was time to go and, at 3.30 p.m., we had perhaps an hour's walking left. Minutes later we bumped into a walker coming up the hill who asked us if we had really been as close to those deer as it seemed.

'Yes,' said Gyan, 'We are their friends!'

'Likely story. I thought you lot would have cut their throats given half a chance!'

'Not today!' laughed Gyan.

Further on we were stopped by a Canadian couple who were slowly ascending in the hope of reaching the summit that day and asked us about the conditions. It transpired that the man was blind. 'You should not go,' advised Dhal abruptly.

'Hell, I just climbed Torridon,' he argued.

'It's midsummer down here, midwinter up there.'

When he learned who we were, he pulled out a fiver for our funds.

'I thought he thought he was on Torridon for a moment!' giggled Dhal, 'And then I thought I'd thank him for twenty pound note, and watch his face!'

The others shrieked with laughter like horrified kids hearing of some dreadful cheekiness. The route now took us down a bulldozer track which ran due east and down to where on the far side of the glen, at the Spittal of Glenmuick, waited Campbell. We were never to solve the mystery of Muick's pronunciation. Some locals swore Muck while others Moo-ick. Perhaps it's like Glenmorangie, where the distillery workers themselves use different versions. Later we were assured that the definitive pronunciation is Loch Mick and that's the one we used.

Gyan was grappling with one of those world-shaking problems. I knew by the face.

'Neil, what is the difference between bravery and being above the call of duty.'

'I suppose, doing something more than what your orders were is above the call of duty.'

'So, you can't be brave fulfilling orders?'

'Well, yeah, I suppose it's a matter of what you did.'

'But all soldiers should be brave, shouldn't they?' Gyan appealed.

'In theory, but true bravery is putting your life at risk to complete a mission or to save colleagues.'

'But isn't that duty?'

'Yes, but bravery is often doing something in spite of your proper fear.'

'There is no such thing as proper fear!' he exclaimed.

'What about the fear for one's life,' I countered.

'No soldier can think like that,' he concluded. Some Gurkha beliefs are inarguable, and as bravery is their main area of expertise, our debate faltered. We never did sort out when something is above the call of duty, and whether carrying out orders could be classed as brave, but it was no mere abstract to Gyan; it mattered. Long after, I discovered that for Gurkhas, unlike British soldiers, bravery awards come with a monthly payment. Although only a small sum, it seems without rhyme or reason to a Gurkha who sees all soldiers as doers of brave deeds. 'Who can understand the ploys of the gods?' they ask philosophically – as do we all of the powers that be.

Soon we were crossing a hot dusty road where on the right was the loch with no correct pronunciation. Victoria and Albert had been rowed around it a number of times, and they had built themselves a 'simple' bothy nearby, which was in fact a sumptuous mini-palace hidden behind the walls of a cottage, where, like Marie Antoinette, they could play at rusticity. Just like any bullying granny, she decided that when Albert died, the bothy never be used again because of its associations with her late husband. Another was acquired which she named 'The Widow's House'. Perversely, nowhere else fell into this category. Her Majesty loved to revisit all the other places she and Albert had enjoyed together, not least Balmoral itself.

While most took advantage of the sun to sit in the car park and feed the flock of half-tame chaffinches, our scholars, Ewen, Dil and Surendra took a moment to visit the natural history museum. They came back with stories, not of badgers or red deer, but with quotes from the visitors' book which had described packs of wolves on Lochnagar, or sightings of bears and other fantastic encounters.

'Did you write anything in it?' I asked.

'Oooh, no,' said Dil all too quickly. One day I'll go back and check that book.

Campbell took us to Banchory, a wealthy Deeside village where on the hill was a hotel, a typical Big Hoose, once the residence of a Victorian gentleman and now owned by The Royal British Legion Scotland. Our rooms were not the grand high-ceilinged affairs of the main building, but small and characterless boxes set to their rear. En suite and clean, however, they perfectly suited our needs. Gyan and I, who always roomed together, quickly unpacked, knowing automatically whose bed and which side of the basin was whose.

'Must phone the wife,' he said, dialling his mobile. It is one of the great regrets to young Gurkhas that their families, bar one posting, must remain in Nepal. The only exception is Brunei, where the Sultan provides houses, schools and hospitals for the wives and kids. It's a testament to their reverence for family that so many Gurkha marriages survive. Gyan, though, as a staff sergeant, was in the privileged position of having his wife and two boys living with him for the rest of his career.

Dhal poked his head round the door. 'We having a drink before supper, Neil Saheb?' Meaning, let's go for a drink now.

'Yeah, tell the boys to meet in half an hour in the bar. While you're here, come in, and we'll write a postcard to Kali,' our colleague from the year before.

As they both leaned over the card, I couldn't help but wonder how these men had absorbed so much in so few years. Neither spoke Nepali as their mother tongue but had learned it at school. Then they joined the Brigade and had to acquire a professional competence in that fiendishly idiomatic and idiosyncratic language, English, while at the same time adopting a new alphabet. The Devanagari script makes predictive text practically impossible on your mobile, but its mastery has other benefits. Who else can read *all* David Beckham's tattoos?

I rang my colleague, Leigh Howieson, in Edinburgh, a long-standing unpaid friend of the Gurkhas. A one-woman admin centre, her communication and computer skills had been vital to the organisation of our trip. She was able to compose and e-mail adverts to the Scottish broadsheets while sifting grain from the postal chaff so that we all knew instantly and exactly how the fundraising side was progressing.

'The running total is now £42,000,' she said, 'Plus we've had some hilarious letters from kids. Listen to this: "My family has always liked the Gurkhas. My granny was a sergeant in the Gurkhas."'

'Oh, right! There must be a Gurkha unit we've never heard of!'

'There's also a lovely painting of an elephant with what I suppose are you lot on its back. Below are the words "Good Luck Gurkhas" signed, rather grandly, by Faye Elizabeth Lipton of Dumfries, aged seven.'

'Where did they get the idea that we're crossing Scotland on elephants? Brilliant PR idea though!'

'There's cards from old ladies with Gurkha links but nearly all of them seem to be from ordinary members of the public who haven't even included their address.'

Our adverts had asked for donors to send £5, which is what the Trust pays per week as a pension to the surviving wartime Gurkhas or their widows. This is normally their only income and represents the difference between a tough survival and utter destitution. We had described it as 'a debt of honour'.

'There's one you'll really like,' added Leigh; 'It's from University of St Andrews Students' Association and simply says 'With Best Wishes – Some of us still understand what a debt of honour means.' Leigh's input was a significant factor; not only was she a contact for journalists, she could dismiss the unimportant to deliver exactly the news the team needed. Every fundraiser needs a Leigh, or you're adrift. Bravo, La Leigh!

Armed with the latest information I was ready to phone Simon Pia at *The Scotsman* and deliver good news. Simon was heartily dismissive of all my complaints but needed good stories to fill the Diary. We made do on a pun about Dread Loch Holidays and the great gates of Stonehaven. All grist to the publicity mill. I was later astonished at how many readers hung on to every scrap – and then posted me all the cuttings. Jim Crumley of *The Courier* had written a whole feature article on us that brought such an avalanche of mail that it became a news story in itself.

Simon had been on leave the week before and I had liaised with his colleague, Michael Wade, who'd reported in a robust and unsympathetic way about my physical limitations ('unfit Embra person') but on one occasion I'd filed copy to Tom Morton in Shetland via his GP wife. He'd described how his fellow columnist, Rab McNeil, had accidentally served as a Gurkha after a hilarious incident involving ten pints of Belhaven Ale while hillwalking in Nepal, and remained a great supporter of our treks, so much so he had to visit South Uist from time to time. Rab's a clever writer, ('Is *clever* okay, Rab?' 'Call me anything you like, Neil, so long as its not derogatory and genetic; my Mum gets annoyed.') but has a stern code about mountaineering, which includes the word 'don't'.

The post had winged other cheques and messages of goodwill. George MacDonald Fraser had sent a handsome donation and words of encouragement, although as a resident of the Isle of Man he couldn't take advantage of the Gift Aid Scheme. As a former member of the 17th Indian Division (The Black Cats), he had fought in the last great battle of the War in Burma, Meiktila, as an NCO in the Border Regiment and needed no nudging as to a debt of honour.

Overleaf. *Left:* **Over the hills and faraway. The route stretches into the distance.**
Right: **The lost boys? No, not yet. Gyan dogged, Ewen relaxed, Dil happy and me happily oblivious.**

Lord Macfarlane of Bearsden is an old friend too, and sent a big sum, being proud of his time in uniform. On the last three occasions I've met him he was wearing his Royal Artillery tie. I asked his wife, Greta, what she thought of the Peter Howsman portrait of her husband that hangs in the Scottish National Portrait Gallery. Her response was as fiery as if she'd just joined the Gurkhas and had a kukri thrust into her hands. A great art critic obviously, and owner of several Peploes too. I suspect she'd do a Clemmie Churchill given half a chance.

I was taken aback one morning on lifting the phone to hear: 'Hello, this is Kirsty Wark.' Her no-nonsense, clever voice is instantly recognisable and is obviously used every time she's on the hunt for information, even from me. 'I need to know why there are Gurkhas without an MoD pension. Can you put something in writing?' This, I realised, was not a good time to point out that I didn't work for the Trust – it would sound as if I were avoiding responsibility – and promised something pronto. She'd already posted a big cheque.

'Before you go,' I added, 'Did you know that your stationery and handwriting are almost identical to Joanna Lumley's?' There was a delighted laugh. Thanks, Kirsty, yet more copy for Simon Pia.

To some Joanna Lumley is a glamorous, famous actress. In Nepalese circles, however, she is known as a graceful and generous benefactor of the Gurkha Welfare Trust and daughter of the extraordinary Major James Lumley, late of the 6th Gurkha Rifles and former Chindit who fought behind Japanese lines in World War II. A recent photo of her attending a reunion in *Parbate*, the Brigade's monthly magazine, was simply captioned 'Joanna Lumley, daughter of Major Jimmy Lumley, 3/6th GR'. As a happy recipient of chatty letters and cards from Joanna, I shamelessly began to put it about that we were old friends. Slightly understandable, but her name was like magic when included in a press quote – and wouldn't you like a letter from La Lumley that described you as a 'hero'? Go on, deny it. Her support was completely genuine and she clearly adores Gurkhas. All the same, when she sent a Christmas card I couldn't help but read aloud the lines of greeting – all morning – to the point where colleagues suddenly pretended they had business elsewhere. It ought to be added that her cheque was the biggest we had ever received and only the Data Protection Act prevents me from printing the figure.

Chandra's piano smile spread from behind a pint. 'Absolutely fabulous!' he grinned. Like many Gurkhas, even if they couldn't speak good English, he was fascinated with new phrases and when he learned that Joanna Lumley had bought one of our jackets, he went away and perfected the catch phrase. Joanna, I realised, was more than just a Trust supporter to the modern Gurkha. She had written that she'd wear the jacket from New York to Milan, and later wrote that it had seen heavy duty service as far east as Bombay.

Another Gurkha friend, Signaller Milan Rai, was to present me with a brocade Buddhist prayer tapestry, a *thangka*, with the words 'Absolutely Fabulous' written in black ink over the raw orange silk of its reverse. My adjectives, such as *glorious, magnificent, splendid* or *wonderful* were repeated with a mix of seriousness and humour that only a Gurkha can master. They're all natural mimics and there is one sapper I know who can point to his chest and, in a Kensington shriek, order: 'On me, chaps!' that brings howling laughter every time.

If the verbs *grin, laugh* and *smile* seem to appear with too great a frequency in this tale, read this by Eric Shipton, who wrote of his Rai porters in the 1930s: 'Their quality is largely due to their robust sense of humour. It hardly ever failed. Each enjoys jokes against himself as delightedly as those who had perpetrated them ... They were forever laughing and chatting together as though they had just met after a prolonged absence.'

The Legion's regulars are always delighted to see serving soldiers in their premises, especially Gurkhas, but here in Banchory they had a curious local habit of letting slip as to how close they were to the Royals, and that etiquette prohibited out-and-out recognition should one find oneself alongside Her Majesty in the bank or supermarket. Almost everyone had a tale of bumping into Prince Charles in the Post Office or Prince Philip in the bakers.

'They live just up the road, you know,' averred one, sotto voce, and that he, for one, treated them as normal, part of the family, you might say.

'I saw Her Majesty in a shoe shop the other day,' confided another. 'Of course, I didn't say anything.' No wonder. Balmoral is fifty miles

Overleaf. *Left:* **Cpl Dil Kumar Rai of 2nd Battalion Royal Gurkha Rifles was Just back from Sierra Leone.**
Right: **Our moon boy, Chandra, taking a rare opportunity not to smile.**

away and the Queen wasn't even in the country. Ah, well, the wish to be special cannot be denied.

My legs stiff, we trotted down to the High Street's Derbah Tandoori for our promised blow out. Peer pressure, rather than written rules, prohibits off-duty Gurkhas from wearing denim, so the boys wore freshly-ironed shirts and sharply-creased chinos. They resembled suitors meeting would-be in-laws, but were unquestionably Gurkhas. Having missed supper the night before, we were due double rations and to hell with the cost. A long table had been set up and we were the centre of attention, attention which happily included that of the staff – one of whom was Nepalese. Rarely does one have true reason to feast, be bloody starving *and* have worked off the requisite calories, but tonight was the night. We hit the food like buses and gorged ourselves like Rabelaisian wolves. Little bowls of *khursarni* were by every place-setting like tempting suicide pills but I knew enough to lay off. Eating is a great unifier and I felt very deeply that right now I was part of an organic unit, a *borg*, and that everyone was part of me and of each other. Unusually for Nepalese, we even had a sweet and then sat rather grandly with liqueurs.

We left and climbed up the hill to our beds, the night not even fully fallen. Just beside the Legion hotel, Gyan brought out a tiny video camera and began filming the building, with the commentary: 'And this is where Staff Sergeant Gyan Bahadur Tamang stayed with his team, having led them over Lochnagar … ' We pushed knuckles into our mouths to stop the laughter. We are *borg*, we are now all unquestionably Nepalese *borg*.

VII

Glen Esk

~~~

In no rush, we dallied over breakfast, able to flick through the papers like real holidaymakers. The lead story in every Scottish title was 'Love Blossoms for SNP Leader' and described how John Swinney had confirmed he was going out with BBC journalist Elizabeth Quigley. 'And to make the relationship official, the couple happily posed for photographs in Edinburgh,' explained *The Daily Record*.

Ewen tapped *The Herald's* big cover picture: 'You know this girl, don't you?

'Er, yes, we used to have lunch together when she was on *The Scotsman*.'

I blinked several times. *The Sun* had a cartoon of Liz reporting from Swinney's bedroom. I even knew John, albeit not very well His uncle, Thomas Peck Hunter, was the only Royal Marine to have received the Victoria Cross in World War II. Alex Ferguson's private Commando museum had included not only a 1944 photo of Royal Marines posing with a signed Nazi flag at Lake Commanchio, Italy, but actually possessed the actual tattered banner. It was a source of huge interest to our men because it was here that Thomas Hunter had died winning his medal. What a coincidence: we'd only just laid our wreath at Spean Bridge too. The boys weren't remotely impressed; Neil Saheb knows everyone, doesn't he? Liz and John were married in 2003, and no, I wasn't invited. Though when I told her this story, Liz had a good laugh.

We quickly found ourselves at the head of Glen Esk, a long valley which pushed down to Fettercairn in the east. The gang was now eating up miles, aware that it would all end the next day and that we faced only a downhill march to the sea. The mighty tendon stretching, muscle burning, was behind us, and ahead was only the sweeping farmscapes of Kincardine. Appropriately, the weather was fair: blue skies and a fresh breeze with a summer warmth. Initially, there was a strange mix of grouse moor on the left and hedge-hemmed sheep country on the right where rabbits zipped and bobbed between thick thistles. The road was lined with sycamore and silver birch above grass and heavy bracken.

'What's that?' asked Dhal, tossing a stone at the object in question. A dozen indignant partridge-like birds scurried through the grass like a group of women trying to maintain their dignity while wearing too-tight skirts. Dhal's stone had landed right in their middle. With outstretched necks and uncertain step, they looked goofily myopic.

'I think they're corncrakes!' I shouted. 'I never knew they were so big. Always thought they were thrush-size.'

'Can you be sure?' cautioned Ewen.

'Fairly. What else could they be?' For a rare bird it is strange how often one hears the phrase 'voice like a corncrake' when so few have actually heard it. The rasping call, like a piece of wood being drawn against a comb, was once a familiar sound, and gives the bird its odd scientific name, *crex crex*. The mystery of the disappearing corncrake is only partially understood, but is probably connected with the changes in the methods and timing of mowing hay. Nineteenth century farmers used to mow a month later and used scythes; given that the corncrake raise their young in the long grass the consequences are obvious. However, this doesn't explain the population collapse to near extinction, and experts believe that there must be another mysterious unknown factor.

Corncrake or no, it meant little to our Gurkhas, though some wildlife certainly caught their attention. 'Snake! Snake!' said Chandra sharply. Sure enough, our Moon boy was directing a two-foot long black adder right down the middle of the road towards us. By putting the point of a stick before the left side of the adder's head and then the right, he was guiding the reptile with unthinking mastery. A two-foot snake when you're not expecting it looks bloody enormous, plus this one was moving with the smooth speed of a cruise missile.

'A black adder! I've never seen one before!' I half yelped as the lads crowded round to inspect the beast, whose body was almost completely black but the darker zigzag down its back was just discernible. Chandra, I noticed, had hardly raised his voice.

'No, don't kill it. Let it go,' I pleaded. There were murmurs of both approval and regret. I'm not sure how evil the snake is in their culture but it's fair to say that this one would have been a goner without my intervention. It's said that all military discipline can evaporate when Gurkhas encounter game, but I was impressed that these men reacted quite coolly. British soldiers would have been leaping into each others' arms. I remember one machine gun group of my fellow countrymen on the Hong Kong-Chinese border flushed by a small python in 1975. The shrieks were girl-like; all that was missing were the pigtails. And the question remains, just how did Chandra 'find' this adder?

Dil and Dhal were scanning the sky, their eyes crinkled against the brightness. Above us circled what were almost certainly buzzards, but was one a golden eagle? It's practically impossible to tell when you're dealing with tiny silhouettes, but it wasn't likely.

'Eagle, Neil? I always wanted to see one in Scotland,' asked Dil.

'Nah, buzzards. You can only tell for certain if a buzzard and eagle are alongside each other and you can tell which is bigger, but you don't get groups of eagles flying together, so we can say these are buzzards.'

'Are there many eagles here?' Dhal suddenly seemed galvanised by the prospect.

'Well, there are some. There's plenty of carrion and rabbits round here, so they won't exactly be starving. In fact, we don't know exactly how many eagles there are in Scotland. There are about four hundred pairs but only half of them breed.'

'The ladies?' asked Chandra, bringing spluttering laughs from Gyan and Dhal. He realised what he'd just said and burst into giggles.

'We don't seem to know very much about some of our national heritage. Like the deer, we know very little about eagles' ranging behaviour, and the number of their nests varies widely. Even the locations of their nests.'

This was listened to with glum puzzlement. Why would Scotland overlook such glorious assets, when it had so much money? It comes as a shock to hear Scotland referred to so often as 'one of the richest countries in the world' because it's so rarely mentioned in our own culture. But it's a fact, as is our ignorance.

'I find rabbit,' said Surendra confidentially, before explaining that he had just come across an injured one, with both back legs broken 'by motorbike'.

'What have you done with it?'

'I left it carefully.' It transpired he'd left it with a banana and cheese sandwich. No one seemed to think this amusing. Will I ever understand these guys?

A short-base Land Rover stopped ahead and a gangling pensioner bounded out. This was a local farmer, a character and former Scots Guardsman, Angus Davidson.

'Heard you were headed this way. Pop into my place, couple of miles on the left, the kettle'll be on!' he greeted, shaking hands all round before departing with a similar energy level. Sure enough, about fifteen minutes later this tall, lean man with a mop of thick white hair, was pouring us tea as we stood around his kitchen, while he gave a non-stop commentary on his life and times. There was a pile of shortbread that disappeared with competition speed that was only just short of downright rude.

'My wife died a year ago, so I live here by myself,' he announced almost enthusiastically, 'More tea anyone?' We were surprised that this energetic man lit up quite so many B&Hs but his life as a sheep farmer had left him athletic and ruddy. Everyone had to sign the visitors' book.

'Was in the Scot Guards. Oh, Mike Gow, Campbell Graham, know the lot,' he elaborated, referring to men who had gone on to be a full general and a major respectively. 'Malaya was my favourite.'

The lads never even sat down, and stood around the kitchen like prep school boys in shorts and earnest expressions. Even their baseball hats looked like school caps. This was an old warrior, one to be respected, a man who had guarded the Queen herself at Buckingham Palace. We read his scrapbooks and fingered the photos feeling we had fallen into a place we would long remember. As we left, he shook our hands as if we had been initiated. A letter of thanks was posted the next day, along with a Gurkha tie.

It was rather too soon but the Glen Esk Folk Museum came round the corner less than an hour later and we couldn't resist.

'Weren't we supposed to meet Campbell here?'

'Yeah, and over there's the vehicle.'

'Gyan,' I said, 'You're the nearest. See if Campbell is in the van.'

After a moment, Gyan reported back that it was empty but just as we were wondering where Campbell could be, a figure rose from the minibus. Gyan's recce had obviously been a wee bit lax.

'I was asleep,' explained Campbell unnecessarily as he stepped towards us as if auditioning for *The Return of the Mummy*.

'No kidding!' we hooted. Gyan blushed at such an elementary oversight for a trained killer like himself. He'd never live this down, and, indeed, he hasn't.

The foyer contained a hundred or so stuffed birds, including kestrel and pheasant.

'Look!' I cried, 'A corncrake! I was right!' Which bird spotter has ever been confronted within an hour with a dead specimen of the disputed sighting? And it was the right size too.

The Museum is run as a small charity and it houses 18th and 19th century agricultural and domestic items from the glen which on first sight you'd never imagine would interest a bunch of Gurkhas. You'd be quite wrong. Although Ewen and I had no idea what were the uses of spiked collars, obscure blades and strange-shaped shovels, these boys did.

'That's for stopping calves from taking milk when they are too old.'

'This knife is for cutting grass that has already been cut.'

'The stone is used for making cloth. My grandmother made my first jacket with one. It's a weight.'

Of course, these boys grew up in an agricultural society which knew and used everything on show. I imagined they could have explained easily the implements that the curators were not sure about. This was an area where they were all well ahead of us. All of them, for instance, knew how to weave a basket, plait ropes from grass and make a halter. Instead of being a museum of old Scotland, it was an insight into a forgotten Nepal. I took a photo of Dil sitting with a manikin of a mother and child before a hearth. You will not believe how comfortable he looks, no matter how incongruous a Gurkha may appear in a 19th century Highland setting.

Part of the excitement was that the Rai's religion, known as Mudum, although influenced by both Buddhism and Hinduism, is centred on shamans, elders and the home. Bear in mind that the Limbu and Rai are collectively known as the Kirat, and that legend has it that they are all descended from a group of brothers (Sherpa, Rai, Limbu, Tharu and Tamang) so that all our boys were culturally linked. Their major annual ceremony, *Puja*, centres on a holy man, a *dhami*, blessing the family house. It should have been no surprise that a museum celebrating hearth and home hit a special chord with these men.

When we had entered a chirpy wee man sat behind the till and when I asked him how much it was to get in, his elderly face spread into a sunburst smile. He knew who we were and refused our money. 'Not after the way we've treated you,' he added sadly, his expression theatrically switching to morose. Somehow he'd charged Surendra, who had been a minute ahead of us, and now stood looking puzzled as we swept in free of charge. I slipped him a couple of pound coins to redress the anomaly, but remembered that this was the guy that had checked out the Glenmuick visitors' centre and was always quietly listening whenever Ewen and I were discussing history.

We left uplifted: a press cutting on the wall told us that the television presenter, John Inverdale, found this place one of his greatest, happiest secrets. There was even a free e-mail facility which had allowed me to send a further report to *The Scotsman* concerning the boys' discovery, along with a notice proclaiming the Tarfside Sheepdog Annual Dance. The only query: why is the glen spelled Glenesk and Glen Esk?

In fact, I knew this glen well. As a seventeen year old I had worked here as a grouse beater for the late Duke of Roxburghe who had paid me, and fourteen others, £15 per week, put me up in comfort and had a French chef serve the meals. Based at Millden Lodge, further down the glen, I had tramped all over this part of Angus with a teenage energy that I can now barely recall.

Money was everywhere. From the gleaming Land Rovers to the titled guns, we saw immense wealth at close quarters like something from *Gosford Park*, with maids, ghillies, chefs and nannies. We even had a Ghillies' Ball in our bunkhouse, complete with the old Duke, Bobo, in burgundy smoking jacket. We were also witness to all that is good about a great country estate, where men cared for the land, fixed fences, stopped erosion and ensured that it reflected their pride.

The work was unforgivingly physical but I thrived among a group of Geordie seasonal workers, teachers and students. The few weeks here, when I'd come off the hill bare-chested, my legs light green with heather pollen, glowing with happiness, have always been at the back of my mind since.

Five years after my time at Millden, I found myself at a supper in London where one girl announced she'd recently had lunch with the Dukes of Westminster and Roxburghe. I couldn't help it. 'And how is

Guy?' I asked, all innocent, 'We used to work together, you know.' It's true that I twice spotted the young Duke-apparent on grouse drives but that was the limit of our association.

Hence when I stood outside our old bothy, my heart both sank and sang. Those golden weeks, long gone. It had begun raining but it failed to dull my memories of flooded sunshine on these same stone walls. In fact, it was dull and empty, like a school you used to attend, but now closed.

'Can I help you?' came a, frankly, less than helpful voice.

I turned and there stood our former head gamekeeper, Dennis Caithness, his hair still dark red. He hadn't put on weight and was possibly wearing the same tweeds from 1973.

'Dennis? I worked here years ago as a grouse beater and was just checking on the old place.'

Dennis was genuinely interested to hear my memories. The estate had long been sold, and its glory days gone. They didn't even shoot grouse here anymore. Like Jack at Corrour, the word 'Gurkha' didn't seem to register when I nodded over at them. Dennis was holding some cans that I knew to be cyanide.

'You're gassing rabbits?'

He laughed as if to say that this was what he was now reduced to. Like me, times had changed. He looked barely a day older, while I was unrecognisable. The poet within me mourned for the boy I had been. The word 'yearn' has a throat-catching edge; I suddenly yearned in the grey rain.

'Corncrake? Are there corncrake here?' I wasn't in a complete reverie.

'Oh, yes, they're coming back. Further up the glen, you'll see a few.'

That was all I needed. As soon as I got back home I helpfully wrote to the *Reader's Digest Book of Birds* pointing out this hitherto unknown development. This was not a madcap campaign, you understand, but I was unimpressed by the editor's curt dismissal that the RSPB disagreed with my sightings. Who do you think informs the RSPB if not the likes of

Overleaf.   *Left·* **Meeting the locals. Kincardine's farms were a revelation after the barren hills of our first six days.**
Right: **Gyan with his Senior NCO expression. Photos were not moments of levity for Gyan.**
Next page. **Chandra surveys a Chinese carryout with unusual grimness.**

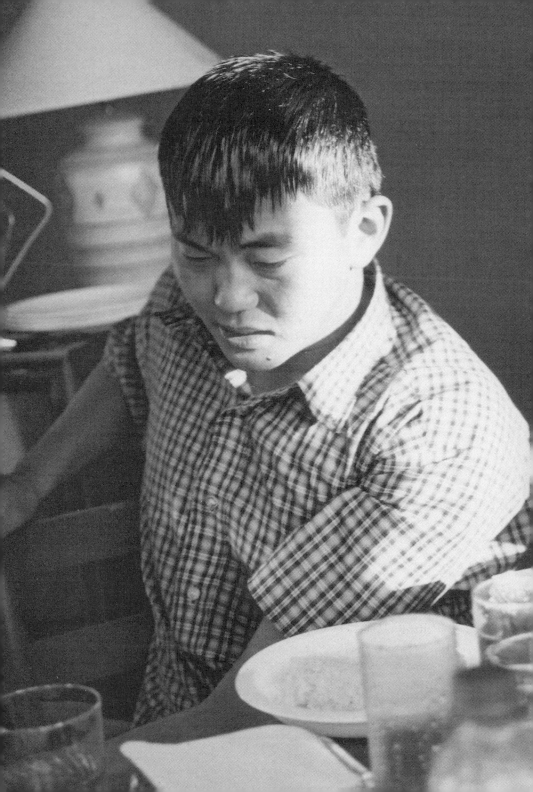

me who had just seen a stuffed corncrake and had chatted to a local gamekeeper?

'Take us home, Campbell!' We arrived back at Banchory embarrassingly early for trans-Scotland hikers, but we had covered the necessary miles and were in danger of finishing a day too early if we kept up the pace.

'What about a game of snooker,' asked Dhal. Gyan picked up the gauntlet and the twosome disappeared to the Legion's big snooker room. 'I'm gonna whip his ass!' Dhal hissed back at us. He lost. Ewen witnessed the game: 'Dhal was too adventurous, Gyan was dead steady, kind of like their personalities.' Ah, yes, snooker and the art of character analysis. Chandra and Surrendra battled over the pool table with equal competitiveness. In their case Surendra was the cool one and Chandra the mad option-taker. Guess who won?

Ewen and I wandered round the town, and took in a summer art exhibition that confirmed that this was a very well-off community indeed, artistic too. Fundraisers will be aware that Scotland, in terms of donors, has a couple of well-known hotspots where the wealthy retire to rural splendour. Banchory is one of these hotspots; we had received an extraordinary number of £100 cheques from its cosy, comfortable houses. We sat in a small café which served up proper home-made rock buns and eavesdropped on the chatter of the wealthy womenfolk who fruit scone which centred on horse and house prices. We liked Banchory for its cool clean streets, its gracious trees and Highland ambience. There was a rising sense of achievement too, the march was nearly over and it looked as if we were going to bring in a record sum for the Trust.

It had been realised in the sixties that some surviving Gurkha wartime pensioners were living in penury, and the Gurkha Welfare Trust was created by their former British officers in 1969 to alleviate the problem. Although 250,000 of the wee men flocked from the high Himalayas to serve the British in World War II, nearly all served for the duration of the war and did not complete the full fifteen years which would have qualified them for a pension. While this is true of nearly all our wartime allies, the Gurkhas fall into a special category, and not least in the affections of the British public. Having served the British Crown since 1815, they are our oldest and best allies, whose word was not bound by short-term promise and self-interest. There are many nations which have shown Britain friendship in the past two hundred years, but none in the Gurkha class.

Just one short story out of countless thousands gives an insight. They first quick marched through the Khyber in 1839, jeered as beardless boys, as part of the disastrous British Army of the Indus, and established a base at Charikar, slightly to the north of Kabul (coincidentally the fort later became home to the BBC's John Simpson before he 'liberated' Kabul from the Taliban all by himself in 2001). When attacked in the 1842 uprising, the Gurkhas were hopelessly outnumbered but resisted with a savage stoicism, then retreated under the cover of darkness. A bugler, too badly injured to escape, sounded reveille and convinced the attackers that the garrison still stood. The two officers, Lts Haughton and Pottinger, got back to India. One became Governor of the Andaman Islands but the other died in Hong Kong of typhus shortly afterwards. The defence of Charikar was never acknowledged by the British authorities. The subsequent murderous retreat to India, apart from the fall of Singapore a century later, is the worst defeat the British have ever suffered. The Kabul garrison of 17,000 was reduced to just twenty men. Even if the Gurkhas had handled themselves honourably, the entire business was so terrible it was best passed over.

The Afghanis have never forgotten. In 1879, when six Gurkha regiments returned in the Second Afghan War, no Pathan mocked. They'd learned the hard way that the wee men were the world's best shock troops. And who is soldiering beside us in Afghanistan in 2004? I once asked a Rai paratrooper how he'd found his 2002 tour. He replied, from the heart and with one word: 'Hard.' Their language skills, too, made them irreplaceably important in the hearts and minds campaign.

They've been everywhere, from the Flanders' mud to the Falklands' snows. In the Second World War they fought in Burma, the Western Desert, Italy and even Greece, and rarely asked for anything. Their legend was magnificently confirmed as the 'happy soldier' who bore any burden.

However, all this time the Gurkhas were officially part of the Indian Army, and when in 1947 India received independence, it was not minded to pay pensions for foreign nationals who had been the instrument of the imperial power. Nepal had never even been a colony, so her troops were not able to take advantage of any Commonwealth settlement as did all the others.

But their merit shone through. In an oafish moment of national embarrassment, Britain realised very late on that to lose India might be careless but to lose a fabulous treasure like the Gurkha Brigade was downright foolish. Four of the ten Gurkha Rifle regiments were taken by Britain as a sort of parting gift to itself, moved to Malaya and included in the British Army for the first time. The decision was taken, unbelievably, one week before independence. Not only did this bring them even closer to the British but in 1957 recruiting depots were permitted for the first time ever in Nepal itself. Whole generations of British officers had been able only to guess at the details of their men's homeland. It was as if we had been recruiting soldiers from a forbidden planet; whole reference books were written based solely on information given by soldiers dreaming of home.

The new Republic of India spotted their potential too, and currently has forty-five battalions of what they describe as Gorkas. The whole of the British Army today comprises only forty battalions, two of which are Gurkhas. Every decade has seen cut-backs, leading to prompt redundancies, many tears, and of course, if fifteen years service were not completed, no pension either. Those in this category who have fallen on hard times can claim a pension from the Trust too.

That surviving wartime Gurkhas receive no pension makes most Scots' blood boil. They were bonny fechters and deserve better. When we needed them, they were there. Now they need our help. They're too old to work but too proud to beg. There is enormous affinity between the two nations: we share the pipes, tartan and are, of course, Highlanders. There are some that say we're both tough wee men who like a good barney, and that Gurkhas are but thrawn Scots of the Himalayas.

Today the Brigade of British Gurkhas (the term 'Brigade' was always a misnomer) has but three cap badges: the Royal Gurkha Rifes, the Queen's Gurkha Signals and the Queen's Gurkha Engineers. There are two demonstration companies, at Sandhurst and Brecon, while the practice of sending Gurkha support companies to beef up under-manned British infantry battalions has ended. In recent years the Gurkhas have served in Iraq, Bosnia and Kosovo where their language skills proved a surprise

Overleaf: *Left:* **Banchory. Navy for the signals, green for the infantry. Best regimental mufti and no silly hair styles.**
Right: **Great plans. Gyan draws the route watched by Dhal, Dil and Surendra.**

bonus here too. The Brigade now totals 3,500 men in an Army of 100,000 but it is always subject to MoD reviews, which one day may see the end of our last living link with the Indian Army and a sparkling part of our military heritage.

Britain's relationship with her Nepalese soldiers borders on one way, but the Trust is a shining example of our country returning some of the loyal service so unaskingly given. Today it runs twenty-three area welfare centres in the remotest parts of Nepal, which dispense pensions, medical services and emergency payments. Staffed by former Gurkhas with impeccable records, the work entails much trekking to verify claims in high-altitude villages, but the system works perfectly. The pensioners walk long distances too: two brothers, aged 93 and 91, recently hiked for five days to pick up their payment. Little had changed in their lives; they were tough young men who had become tough old men.

There are 10,400 pensioners, with 3,500 dependant wives, and 5,000 widows, while the administration costs in Nepal are met by the British Ministry of Defence. This means that donations go directly to the needy. It should not be forgotten that there are 25,000 former Gurkhas in receipt of an MoD pension, who served the requisite fifteen years, and find that their pension goes far in their homeland, especially when converted to rupees. Although the Trust needs £270,000 each and every month, there is a bright side: if we all pull together this situation can be resolved. It is not the usual Third World off-the-scale disaster that is beyond both comprehension and solution. With a little bit of commitment it can be worked out.

My legs ached as if I'd been on a Himalayan trek. 'I hope these old buggers are genuinely in dire straits, because I'm going to end up a needy ex-Serviceman too!'

Ewen gave me his usual withering look: 'I've got no problem with my knees,' he sniffed, as if mine were my own fault, the consequence of a dissolute lifestyle which could elicit no sympathy.

The boys were dressed up in regimental mufti for supper: rifle green blazers for the infantry, navy for the Signals, with white shirts and regimental ties. There was no Brylcreem, and silly hairstyles had been forsaken for old fashioned side-partings, as if their mothers had overseen the preparations. It was the Legion's bingo night and we were on show behind a stall of Gurkha goodies to sell to the expected crowds.

Sure enough, a hundred women came pouring through the portals, picking up the teddy bears, tea towels, key rings, miniature kukris and notebooks as if this were a summer sale. Most didn't actually want or need anything, but were anxious to buy something as a donation and show solidarity. Surendra and Chandra, with shy smiles, stuck GWT labels on everyone, supervised by Gyan, who was also overseeing me and Dhal at the sales table. Ewen and Dil were on stand by, a role they took very seriously, to the point that they went off to the bar to think about it.

'Can I buy you?' asked one lady.

'Everybody's got their price,' laughed Gyan, 'How much are you offering?'

The whoops and giggles this created continued all evening, so that grinning women regularly came over to inspect our dashing staff sergeant and ask if he had an hourly rate. You can sell anything with the right attitude; we had bags of it and were nearly sold out. Eventually, a deathly hush fell on the hall as the women took their seats. Was this a Legion Two-Minute Silence? I didn't dare count up the cash for fear of discovering I'd suddenly gone totally deaf. Then came a male voice: 'Two fat ladies, eighty-eight.'

Clearly the mental rigours of bingo require total concentration and there was no chance of doing any further business, so we went off for supper in the Legion's excellent restaurant. I recommend it. Well fed, my bed called early and I left the lads crowing and shouting at their usual last port of call, the pool table: pockets full of wry.

Even the stairs were hard work. Please, God, let my knees survive and I promise I'll never do anything as daft as this again.

Overleaf. *Left:* **Surendra fools around with, not a phone, but a radio as Chandra looks on. Dil is videoing in the background. A blonde is cycling her way up the hill** ...
Right: **Not far now. The sea is on the horizon.**
Next two pages. *Left:* **Always time for food. Perhaps Tesco will commission us to make an advert?**
Right: **Complete portrait. Dhal cool, Surendra relaxed, Dil debonair, Chandra gleeful, Gyan serious and Ewen snow white.**

VIII

To the Sea

~~~

It was midmorning and we stood like blowing elephants, shifting and grimacing. We'd come storming up a minor road, through wheat fields in full summer harvest, and now stood on the brow looking down at Stonehaven which shimmered in a heat haze with the North Sea behind it a dazzling silver. Having driven within sight of the sea yesterday, this was not our first glimpse, and the moment of triumph was not one of heart-jumping elation. Furthermore, we were ahead of ourselves, and with a welcoming committee not ready for an hour, were obliged to take a break.

A blonde girl on a pushbike came slowly labouring up the hill, her head down. Either it was a wish to communicate with a pretty girl or just a happy moment, but Chandra leapt out in front of her, enthusiastically announcing: 'Good morning, Miss. How do you do?' The bike wobbled and nearly crashed. The girl said nothing but regained composure and cycled off. We watched open-mouthed. Chandra looked back at us, embarrassed and gave a nervous smile. The team burst into delighted laughter.

'Nice one, Chandra!' called Ewen, as Surendra and Dil began re-enacting the scene, with exaggerated eye rolls and mimes of thrashing handlebars. Dil thought he had captured the scene on video but, alas, he hadn't.

A big rubbish truck braked and two men got out. 'Gurkhas? Here's a fiver!' They'd read about us and somehow recognised our little group. Handshakes all round and then away: a simple moment of friendship that was the hallmark of everyone we met, and defined the whole trip. It's a fact: everyone we met radiated goodwill and generosity. Shopkeepers, members of the British Legion, the public, (nearly all) hoteliers and even bin men seemed to have inhaled some class A drugs the moment before we came round the corner.

Campbell had joined us but was going ahead to set up the Gurkha goods stall outside Stonehaven's British Legion club. Our trip would have been impossible without his help. While the rest of us all found time to have little moans about the day's injustices, Campbell never did and no chore was too footling. Admittedly, Campbell was thoroughly enjoying himself, but then, so were we all.

He had dumbfounded the lads by announcing that he must buy a coming-home present for his dog, 'Otherwise it'll be devastated.' Ewen and I took a long time to convince them that this was not a joke, though Campbell's plans to build in his home 'a Rangers' Room' as a sort of domestic shrine to the gods of Ibrox gave us further concern for his sanity.

'What exactly will you do in your Rangers Room,' asked Dil, genuinely intrigued by this unexpected religious behaviour.

'Well, I can just go in and look at all my Rangers' memorabilia; it's somewhere to keep them.'

'But what will you *do*?'

'He'll be praying Rangers beat someone – and hoping that Celtic get beat by anyone!' put in Ewen.

Keen football fans, the boys giggled. As rifle green is the Gurkha colour, there is a substantial Celtic following in the Brigade, a fact that can cause a horrified silence in the wrong Scottish quarter. However, the same folk are always delighted and relieved to hear there's a big Rangers' camp too. Another Gurkha-Scotland link.

I leaned over the fence to grab some ripe oats watched by Dhal and Chandra. 'Bran?' asked Chandra. 'Er, no, not bran. Oats!' Although our boys were pretty hot on plant identification, some guesses were more speculative than others. I explained how bran isn't actually a crop but couldn't find the right word in Nepali. Gyan and Dhal frowned in the sun, making terse suggestions only for the other to dismiss them. It took a long time to establish that the word *jau* can mean both barley and oats. Although all the boys enjoyed new words, Chandra always went too far and would, with magnificent self-assurance, ask a waiter for 'legumes'. The waiter's face was always priceless. 'Legumes? Whitza lad sayin'?' Meanwhile Chandra would surreptitiously look round to see how this impressive foray into the English language had gone down with his fellow diners. That his dictionary failed to warn that some words were not in common usage, was never going to inhibit such a boulevardier as he. Other misunderstandings are simpler. Once I saw a Gurkha being asked if he wanted a starter. There was a blank look from our lad. 'You know, like a prawn cocktail.' 'Oh, cocktail!' the light dawning. 'Yes, please, malt whisky, thank you.'

Nepal has a population of over 22 million people but has nearly twenty ethnic groups and more than thirty indigenous languages, so I had to keep on my toes to ensure that the lads weren't giving me their own words or dialect when I needed a translation. Dhal confused me for years by referring to 'my language' and then giving me a totally different vocabulary lesson.

'Nepali is spoken as a second language by about half the people in Nepal,' explained Gyan, 'Though it is used in parts of Bhutan,' he added importantly.

The Tibetan-speaking tribes are called Bhotes, or southern Tibetans, I remembered. Bhot is their word for Tibet and, Bhutan, which lies at the southern edge of Tibet means 'End of Bhot'. In fact, Sherpa means 'man of the East' (*pa=man*). When the Tibetan-born Tenzing Norgay, aged nineteen, joined Eric Shipton in 1935, his name was Tenzing Bhotia. Almost all Nepali words relating to Buddhism, be they prayer flags or shrines, are Tibetan, but strangely there is no word for Buddhism in Tibetan! Buddhists are either *chos-pa* (man of *chos*, the karma or Universal Law) or *b'on-pos* (men of *b'on*). It surprises some to learn that the Lord Buddha – the Awakened One – was born in what is now Nepal, in the 6th Century BC.

His philosophy still fascinates. 'Is it the flag that moves? Is it the wind? Neither. It is your mind.' This is the kind of gem that came from a Buddhist patriarch a thousand years ago and is still treasured. And one of their slogans is 'In clarity unite!' Be aware. Gurkhas often think like this.

Gyan had sent me a photo of his father's death shrine, which was set high on a hillside set round with prayer flags blowing from tall bamboos. Passing away in his nineties, he had seen few changes in his homeland. As a farmer his valley had provided a brutally difficult environment in which to scrape a living. Theirs is a land without roads, a world of steep hillsides without pack animals up which every scrap of building material and every imported foodstuff must be transported by hand. The villages may be as high as 12,000 feet (3,700 metres) where winters are bitterly cold, and most folk reach their late teens without having seen a car. The soil is thin and blown away by arid winds, subject to landslips in the monsoon or when glacial rivers burst their banks and whole hamlets can be swept away. Only a handful of crops can grow, and create a diet of turgid monotony. This is no Shangri-la.

The people have adapted to the rarefied air, the perishing climate and the crushing hardships by revelling in all life's small joys when they come along, so that no happiness is too minor to go uncelebrated. The pleasures of friendship and families are cherished, and every occasion is one marked by good fellowship. Laughter has become an integral weapon in the fight to survive. A smile says I'm alive, I'm making it, I am favoured and the gods are good. And when things are bad, they must be accepted with a shrug. The greatest mountains in the world have brought forth the unquenchable; the untameable has produced the indomitable. And their sons were standing with me on a rise to the west of Stonehaven.

'Let's grab a bite here,' I said. Dil was giving an exhibition of the drill he'd taught the newly-formed army in Sierra Leone, which involved a curious double stamp which seemed to incorporate a certain African exuberance. Chandra and Surendra were discussing how they disliked guarding the Channel Tunnel, mostly because the refugees smelled.

'If you'd been on the run across Europe for weeks, you'd smell too,' chided Ewen.

'Ah. But is terrible,' repeated Chandra screwing up his face. There was a fierce argument in Nepali which I couldn't follow and which ended with a finger-wagging Chandra laughing 'Extra duties! Extra duties!' in English. Almost all military terms are in English, I remembered, even 'chinstraps'.

Beneath the blue skies, it was too hot to eat, and I put away my sandwiches. 'Sandwiches were invented by the Earl of Sandwich, you know, Gyan!'

Gyan looked at me, half smiling, not certain whether I was joking. 'It's true,' I continued. 'He wanted a snack that he could eat while playing cards.'

'And I suppose the Earl of Mar invented the Mars Bar?' he replied. Oh Gyan, you always were bloody quick.

'No, but until recently there was an English law lord called Lord Salmon of Sandwich!' There was a burst of disbelieving laughter. 'It's true!'

At last, it was time to move off. We could see the finish and were set on completing the route with a brisk march of three miles, all downhill to the harbour and with minimum delay. The whole travelling circus was on the move again, on this occasion, however, for the last time. A large fly-over took us above the busy Perth-Aberdeen A94 and we tramped through the gritty streets following the signs to the town centre. In our bright red shirts, shorts and packs, we drew few stares, and passed a long line of North Sea service companies before swinging down to the main square. A large drop of rain hit me on the head.

'Look at that!' Ewen cried, 'Where did they come from?' turning to see the sky was filling with the blackest of clouds.

'From the West!' grinned Gyan.

With barely two hundred yards to go the sky opened and torrential rain poured down, covering roads instantly in sheets of water and filling gutters with bouncing silver streams. The drains, now wide awake, gurgled thirstily. It was suddenly dark, and the townsfolk were hurrying, half bent, from doorway to doorway. So much for our day of glory! It looked suspiciously like we had brought the weather with us. Turning into the main square, we could see Campbell frantically loading the vehicle with armfuls of sales goods. We jogged over to help.

'You know something. What everybody really wanted to buy were those bloody antlers,' gasped Campbell, lifting a large box and indicating with his chin those that were visible in the van.

There was a small jovial crowd of well-wishers in the British Legion who gave a great cheer when we entered. Even more hospitable was the man who took our drink orders at the door, complete with notepad and pencil. It could only have been midday but we sat behind our beers feeling guilty. The long march had ended in undemanding ease, while the crunching miles of Knoydart, Ben Alder, Glen Feshie and Lochnagar seemed so long ago as to be from another trek. But we were here, and just to prove it, we sank a pint of lager in the Royal British Legion Scotland Stonehaven Club.

The Club chairman, George Swapp, made a quietly-spoken, eloquent speech, describing Britain's debt of honour to our friends in Nepal and presented us with a welcome cheque. Not only that, he was going to take us to a nearby café that served the best fish and chips in the world.

My return words of thanks were heavy on how no town in history had been so eagerly awaited as this North Sea fishing port. This was a community of fame and decency, so much so that Lord Reith himself had made Stonehaven his title. There was a further Gurkha link: the town's famous Hogmanay fire festival was much akin to Nepal's Dipavali, Festival of Lights, and we really must be invited back to show how it's done. It was a modest speech, the words didn't come properly but were full of feeling.

An ancient Merchant Navy mariner stopped me afterwards and pushed out an old tobacco tin. 'I didn't know who to give this to, but thought you'd be the right man,' he said, explaining. 'I collected these from all over the world but they've lain in my house all these years, and I thought I'd give them to you.'

I opened the tin to discover a handful of dirty coins and a tight wad of ancient, crumpled banknotes. The latter were from the Seychelles, Iran, Ceylon and India, but there were five crisp one-rand notes from South Africa, dated 1953. Obviously, I was the very man for these! Having no idea of their worth, but suspecting (rightly) very little, I knew they were of enormous value to this old man and thanked him as if they were pieces of eight.

Her Majesty's press were making urgent signs and the team assembled outside in the rain and quick-marched the hundred yards to the shore, a piper leading the way. Shoppers stopped to stare, and I felt uncertain as to whether to wave back or pretend that this was the sort of thing that happened to me all the time and should be taken in my stride.

It was still raining when we reached the sea, but at last the end of our journey was reached and the moment was one to savour. We shook hands knowing that we had completed everything we had set out to do, and done it together. There had been days of sunshine and Shakespeare's 'rainy marching in the painful field', we'd slogged through Knoydart's Commando country, hammered across the Highlands and tramped through the gentle slopes of Kincardine. Without my merry men this would have all been a good idea unlikely to have ever happened, but with a cause and their company, we had pulled it off – and had the best week of the year into the bargain. With anyone else, the two hundred miles would have seemed tougher, drabber, and unlikely to have included quite so much hilarity. I felt deeply grateful to these unassuming, happy, dependable lads.

It is the normal lot of a leader to develop a team's unity, to settle disputes and to ensure that everyone keeps up. This was not mine; my men found every day one big laugh. I was the only squabbler, and who else was going to straggle? All the same, today was on the list of my top-twenty days ever, the times of my life. Though not tired, I was literally bone weary; my knees were approaching their first million mile service and needed rest. The patron saint of quality footwear was due a quick prayer. None of us had so much as a blister, which tells us that the 'thin' boots problem was properly solved back in Edinburgh. Gyan's early difficulties of road-walking in trainers had never re-occurred, but my faithful boots were soon to be thrown out. I had walked a straight thousand miles in them, perhaps more, and they were, literally, on their last legs.

One of the team photos caught exactly every individual's personality, with Dil debonair, Dhal cool, Surendra relaxed, Gyan comporting his features into that serious senior NCO look while Chandra's bright smile shone with uninhibited glee. It was not so much a representation as a proper portrait.

'Can you all jump into the sea, and perhaps frolic a bit?' asked one of the photographers. Frolic? Jump into the sea? Gyan gave him his stern staff sergeant's once over and the idea was quickly dropped. Most press snappers demand several hundred pictures, and digital cameras have made the process easier. If the press ever comes round, give ten minutes for every one they ask for or they'll be disappointed, no matter what their initial request. This was no exception and, though slightly bedraggled, we beamed the biggest smiles in the North East over twenty minutes as opposed to the requested two.

Newspaper photographers were ever thus. The BBC correspondent Kate Adie once helped me by promoting a GWT fundraiser in Edinburgh (and her book, *Kindness of Strangers*) by posing for the press with a uniformed Gurkha rifleman. They stood side by side smiling and all went fine until, after fifty photos, one snapper asked: 'Kate,' (like he'd known her all his life) 'Could you sit with him on the sofa, arm in arm? Or perhaps with his arm round you?'

After a moment's silence, there was a very firm: 'I don't *do* sitting.'

'What about wearing his hat?'

'That is his uniform, and I respect that!' Kate replied in a voice that invited no debate.

A mystified look crossed the rifleman's face – of the normally impassive Pun clan, something was going on that he didn't understand. In fact, the photocall was threatening to descend into quite a newsworthy contretemps. It resolved itself only when it dawned on the photographer that this wasn't Samantha Fox visiting the troops. It might be simple, but my first tip to aspiring pressmen is: don't ask Kate Adie to flirt coquettishly in a Gurkha hat. Personally, I wouldn't have dreamt of pushing Kate Adie around in the first place, never mind asking her to vamp it up. There must be a special minus-intelligence category for some snappers.

I liked Kate very much, and gave her a gold-plated crossed kukris badge which she immediately fastened to her dress. Jadbahadur Pun, our model, was from Pokhara which she had visited but even more impressively had interviewed Prince Charles there. I'd forgotten she had been a royal correspondent.

'Yes, in the middle of it, I realised that either Prince Charles was growing or that I was shrinking. When I looked down, sure enough, my feet were several inches under the mud, and I was sinking!' Prince Charles is both Colonel-in-Chief of the Royal Gurkha Rifles and Patron of the Gurkha Welfare Trust and takes both roles very seriously. The Gurkhas, in return, respect him greatly, so that to have met HRH is an event of great honour. Jad, I'm glad to say, knew exactly who Kate was and was further impressed that she had covered the Gurkhas' entrance into Kosovo and could remember a few names.

'There was a Sergeant Tara,' she recalled.

'*Tara* means star,' I said.

'How appropriate, he saved my life. And how did you learn Gurkhali?'

'Er, from them,' I stumbled, pleased that the famous Kate Adie wanted to know about little me.

When I took my pictures, I didn't try any daft novelty shots, and the thing was done in ten exposures (yes, old fashioned film, I'm afraid), but nevertheless one appeared in *The Scotsman* under the headline *No Sitting Target* – a witty reference to how Kate doesn't pose flung over armchairs.

Overleaf. *Left:* **My picture of Kate Adie and Jadbahadur Pun.**
          Right: **1945 Gurkha Signallers, complete with heliographs, at Hardwar, India.**

Meeting such individuals is another pleasure of helping promote the Gurkha Welfare Trust. Do you think Kate Adie and I would have ever met, never mind swapped stories, without their catalytic force?

'Right, that's all you're getting,' warned Dhal in his sinister sergeant mode, as the rain continued to lash down on the shingle. The snappers weren't entirely sure whether he was threatening, joking or merely making an announcement. The rest of us grinned to ourselves. In my mind's eye, Dhal is always my height and it's always a surprise to see photos which show him to be much smaller.

Our shoreline pressmen finally had their fill. It was time for lunch and we trooped over to a beachfront café that was either a brilliant homage to the 1950s or the owners had seen little reason to redecorate since Buddy Holly first hit the Wurlitzer. We took our plastic seats and tapped the formica tables in awe, genuine, circa 1956, half expecting the waiter to be Stonehaven's reigning King of the Teds. Our lads were oblivious to the extraordinary décor and frowned at the menu.

'What's Cullen Skink?' asked Dil.

'A thick soup of potato and smoked haddock,' I replied.

Our host, George Swapp, a tall slim man in his late sixties, added: 'It's their speciality! When Mel Gibson made *Hamlet* at Dunnotar Castle he brought Glenn Close here to sample some.'

My mind reeled. Mel Gibson and Glenn Close? In here? But a scrap of memory came in flashback: Glenn Close had played Gertrude – and, yes, it was filmed at nearby Dunnotar. But what on earth would big Hollywood stars be doing in here? I looked round at our fellow diners, mostly obese kids stuffing their swollen faces with high fat 'meals' and swilling it down with sweet drinks from appropriately over-sized bottles. This was, I hoped, a preliminary before they all fell into a sugar-induced coma and gave me and the likes of Mel Gibson a bit of peace. The contrast between the five sturdy Gurkhas, blooming with health and flashing white smiles, and the pasty-skinned teenagers was damn near an indictment of the Scottish Health Department.

'Of course, the place was hired privately and they had it to themselves,' explained George. No kidding.

I was now in a serious quandary. Not being especially hungry, but particular to Cullen Skink – the place's speciality – I am also incapable of resisting fresh haddock in bread crumbs, described here as 'the best in the world'.

Dil and Gyan twisted their mouths, sucked their teeth, and ordered both the fish 'n' chips and skink, and Dhal joined them. This was, of course, not gluttony, but a cultural experience, practically educational. Hoping it might be more permissible if Ewen joined me in two courses, I asked what he was having. He pursed his lips, hummed, and said almost speculatively: 'Cullen Skink, then the fish and chips.'

'Two courses?' I boggled. 'Oh, go on then. I think I'll join you.'

George was a pleasure to talk to, and was proud of his town, home to Scotland's last outdoor heated swimming pool in which he'd swum that very morning. It was good of him to offer us this lunch too but he insisted that he and his friends wanted to do something for us, and was proud to be part of this whole endeavour. I spotted him not long ago on a TV quiz, and he accounted well for himself then, just as today he did us proud. He was correct about the food too, both fish and skink were perfect. All that was needed was a brisk hour to walk it all off.

Campbell released the handbrake and we all prepared to doze home, but first stopped at Dunnotar Castle on Stonehaven's southern edge, a magnificent coastal ruin, for a proper look at Scottish culture, as opposed to current culinary trends involving deep fat fryers.

I could see why Mel Gibson chose it. Standing on a promontory with the North Sea washing round the surrounding rocks, it was a ghostly spectacle of past glories and like all castles was only built where hot blood was spilled and men died. It looked straight from central casting, Spooky Old Castles Dept. Cromwell had besieged it in 1652, when it alone held out for Charles II, but it soon fell. The Scottish regalia were only saved by the ingenuity of two women who escaped with the precious items under their skirts. After the Union of 1707 the regalia were put in a chest and did not see the light of day until 1818 when they were discovered by, of all people, Sir Walter Scott. Today they are housed in Edinburgh Castle and although there are older crowns, the collection is Europe's oldest set of regalia. As for Dunnotar vaults, in 1685 Covenanters were imprisoned here under dreadful conditions.

Overleaf.   *Left:* **To trek or not to trek. Ewen and Dil recreating Mel Gibson's Hamlet at Dunnotar Castle.**
Right: **Dunnotar Castle.**
Next two pages. *Left:* **It's raining, it's pouring, but we've made it to the North Sea.**
Right: **What the well-dressed Gurkhas are wearing this summer. Waiting to enter Stonehaven.**

Returning to the vehicle, Gyan was inspired, like a clan bard, to have a shot at reciting his country's history from the minibus's front seat. 'Civilization was blossoming in Nepal before the fifth century BC … ' At this point he turned round to discover all his charges were determinedly asleep.

The history of the world's only Hindu kingdom sets it apart from every country on the planet, and, unusually, its early days are integral to how it is ruled today. Buddhism did indeed surface in the 6th century BC, and there then followed twenty-eight successive kings, a tradition that is hard to shake. Around 300 AD the Indian Licchavi dynasty invaded, introducing Hinduism and the caste system. This intermingled with Buddhism, a process that continues today. Almost uniquely, Nepal has never had any religious wars. The 1400s left a wealth of architecture, carvings and sculpture but in 1768 the princely kingdom of Gorkha conquered the Kathmandu Valley and began a dynasty that continues to this day.

Until 1948 Nepal had remained a forbidden kingdom, a romantic phrase that brought no material blessings. The first elections were in 1957 but the country remained in the grip of fierce feudalism. Two years later the King arrested the entire cabinet and introduced a system of locally elected village councils to nominate candidates for higher posts, all ultimately under the king, and endorsed by the Eton-educated King Birendra when his father died in 1972. It was this monarch that re-introduced proper elections in 1991. The kingdom has now had democracy for fifteen years and little to show for it. The tradition of Nepal's rulers living in luxury led to rampant corruption which no ruling politician wanted to change.

In June 2001 the Crown Prince killed his whole family before turning the gun on himself and took two days to die. His uncle, Gyanendra, ascended but the problems accelerated. Bonded labour was abolished only the year before but 90% of the population lives off the land with the majority existing at subsistence level. It is a very hard life, with the average annual per capita income a mere $150. The prospects for children are indescribably bleak. Nepal's astronomical birth rate, lack of arable land and destruction of forests means disaster is inevitable.

Nepal is barely industrialised. With no manufacturing base, all machinery and construction materials must be imported, and paid for in hard currency. One of the main sources of this currency is from Gurkhas, while foreign aid programmes provide a third of Government revenue.

The root of the problem is the spiralling population. The 1950 five million figure has jumped to 22.6 million and is expected to double in the next thirty years. Almost the whole nightmare has been created by Nepal's wilfully self-serving ruling class, who constantly call for change but refuse to implement any.

The only organisation prepared to address the monumental corruption and criminal mismanagement are the Maoists whose movement began a 'People's War' in 1996 with the doomed intention of over-throwing the state. Given that the grievances were well grounded, many supported them so that today the majority of the seventy-five districts are in their hands. The tactics are simple: attack isolated police posts and assassinate any passing politician. Not surprisingly, this has been a disaster for the ordinary people, adding to the other human tragedies that are unfolding around them. Life has become doubly hard. Security measures have been heavy-handed, while Maoists can bully and extort the helpless with little fear of retaliation.

Although serving Gurkhas visiting their home villages are subject to demands for cash, up to £500 per trip, the Maoists treat the GWT pensions as a form of socialism and have never attempted to appropriate them, though roadblocks and security checks can slow down the distribution. Despite the circumstances, this is very good news. If the Trust could not assure donors that their money is going unmolested to the needy, then income would be seriously affected. Nevertheless, Maoists taking over Nepal is the very last thing its impoverished people need. The already limited wealth would disappear completely along with attendant human rights. It would spell an end to the British Gurkhas too, and quite how Maoists in power would regard insulting hand-outs from former imperialist overlords remains to be seen. In short, the future, though not completely black, looks dark.

Neither Gyan nor Dhal wanted to return to Nepal upon discharge. It was not just the fear of having their hard-earned savings appropriated by some teenage commissar but the whole convulsive switch to a near medieval existence that concerned them. A Gurkha captain, whose

Overleaf. *Left:* **Surendra surveys the tea pot he has just filled with mineral water.**
Right: **The over-thoughtful Surendra wondering what next!**

children had been born in Hong Kong and raised in England, told me of the time he took his teenage daughters back to their home village. They were disgusted. 'But this is your heritage,' he'd pleaded, aware how plaintive his voice sounded when explaining that they'd soon get used to the absence of electricity and lavatories.

Gyan also felt deeply that he would be letting down his two sons, aged twelve and fourteen, who were doing brilliantly at the local school in Dorset. The inability to acquire either a work permit or British passport was another subject where burning resentment lay just below the otherwise calm Gurkha surface.

'When we walk down the street, we see people of all colours, some nothing to do with Britain, all living here,' said Dhal, his voice trailing off.

'We have served the Crown for twenty years, but are sent back to Nepal like we had done something wrong, while all these others get to live here,' added Gyan. The unspoken message was that Gurkhas feel hard done by. We're talking of about 180 Gurkhas leaving the Army every year. Can't Britain give passports to the proportion that would like to receive them – as a just reward for service to the country? It's not as if they are disreputable characters. We gave one to Zola Budd in two minutes, less time than it would take her to run 3,000 metres, even if she had stayed on her feet for the whole race.

Though Gurkhas have all sorts of clan links, there is now an unseen telephonic web that draws them even closer together. Once, when I needed to contact a Pun sergeant, I asked a Pun corporal who, via a Pun rifleman, gave me the number within minutes.

The trip back to Edinburgh transformed the van into a mobile telephone exchange as the boys rang up countless fellow Gurkhas to tell them of their heroic exploits in the Scottish Highlands. The mighty warriors had conquered every peak in the country, it would appear from hearing their chatter. Incoming calls lit up their phones – nothing but the latest model, of course – with a variety of ring tones. Gurkhas have never heard the words 'false modesty' and are comically sentimental. They have been known to wax lyrical about the good old days in recruit training the very day after they had passed out.

When we pulled up outside my flat, it was as if we'd triumphed on Everest itself, and garlands and hosannas were our due. In fact, it was time for a feast from the local Chinese carry-out and bed, but not before reliving those heroic moments atop Lochnagar and the famous victories in Knoydart. Fatigue hit us all a wee bit earlier than usual, a fact announced by Dhal who suddenly grunted in Nepali that he wanted us out of his bedroom. Everyone disappeared like rabbits.

The trip was not over yet. Tomorrow held exciting attractions in Scotland's capital, our own celebration and at least one big surprise. I went out like a switch had been thrown.

Edinburgh and Home

~~~

You'd think it was a peculiarly Western vice, but you'd be wrong. Don't laugh: Gurkhas love shopping for clothes but it's got to be top clobber and none of the cheap stuff that you get in all the chain stores. I once came across three of them in a Princes Street shop trying on all the gear with comic self-admiration, hands on hips, turning this way and that as they took in their reflection, whilst making some very un-Gurkha-like noises of approval. I knew one of them, a corporal, and said 'hello'. We chatted for a moment, but he continued zipping and unzipping his jacket, barely taking his eyes from the mirror just like a true fashionista.

Surendra, in particular, had a collection of shirts which were stylish, tasteful and obviously not cheap. Frankly, I've come across too many young soldiers who consider themselves fashion experts from the moment they buy their first suit. Nowhere was this more obvious than in Hong Kong where soldiers were permitted to design their own wardrobe. If baggy trousers are the thing, then let's add a yard to the measurement. Are waistbands with four buttons fashionable? Then let's have five! One soldier dreamed up a Gestapo leather mac complete with a collar of diced black and white rabbit fur. The cuddly gangster on hallucinogens look never took off, but every girl did – on sight. For legal reasons we cannot name the designer, a diminutive bridegroom who skated up the aisle in six inch heels that resembled orthopaedic boots and whose emergency stop employed the best man as crash barrier. Few could forget the suede sports jackets which, with just a slight elbow movement, had the lapels twitching like gull wings.

With no sartorial experience young soldiers lunged in, knowing that if nothing else, the results would be special, perhaps unusual, but always unforgettable. The fearless, brave and tasteless wore loud checks, while the unexpected detachment of whole arms indicated the gullible, the inexperienced and the plain stupid. The only restraints were the limits of the soldier's imagination which is why one came across blazers with red buttons and brocade cuffs. In the 1970s it was not unusual to see some eighteen year old tramping down Nathan Road in a Prince of Wales check splendour, the padded shoulders prohibiting entrance to smaller doorways, with flares flapping like flags and with a waistband that resembled a waistcoat. The ensemble made tout by two-tone golfing brogues. I know, I was that soldier. Barmen would ask: 'What have you come as?'

Gurkhas, I'm delighted to say, fall into this category and a day in Edinburgh's up-town shops called with an irresistible allure. Gyan and I stayed at my flat, reading the papers, while the others charged off to check out the city's rag trade.

'Strange how all these young men suddenly adapt to our ways,' I said aloud.

'Not really. When you are keen to have something, learning is no problem. Even technology is no problem. We all have e-mail addresses,' replied Gyan. Why did this bring me up short? It was like the time I apologised for the sleeping arrangements: 'We are soldiers, Neil.' The same gentle reminder of the obvious. Though I'm past the quill and parchment stage, and can actually use parts of my computer, I'm tempted to believe that iPods have something to do with peas and that broadband applies to the top of my trousers. But these boys have got phones that are way above my ken, and sussed out my GPS in ten seconds, despite me not being absolutely happy with it after ten months. Then it dawned: they're more sophisticated than me.

At breakfast Chandra had described how the Battalion was headed for Brunci, 'All hot and dirty, not like Shorncliffe,' referring to 2RGR's current base in opulent Kent. 'You would like Brunei perhaps. It's a biological paradise!'

Their wish to be colloquial often didn't produce the intended results, but it reflected a driving hunger to communicate. Their monthly magazine, *Parbate*, usually contains some gems that ought to appear in a fundraising volume. This is how those executed in the First World War were described: 'British warriors who had great offences were kept in a cell and were sacrificed the next morning.' Well, nearly. One sergeant wrote to me, regretting his unavailability for another trans-Scotland trek with: 'I will have to abandon my desires this year,' which promises more than it delivers, me thinks.

But they loved puns. Dhal had defused a moment of earlier frisson when Gyan had assumed that someone else was going to prepare his breakfast and was sitting hurrumphing. Dhal had suggested that our most suitable cereal should be *Ready Trek* which everyone howled at.

The boys returned mid afternoon with bulging bags and the casual disdainful pride of fashion-shoppers, but were either loudly or quietly thrilled to handle the waiting hundred or so 6x9-inch photos of the trip. Boots the Chemist had kindly provided the service free of charge thanks to their Scottish PRO Jane Robertson: a set for every member of the team! In fact, Boots had offered free sun cream too, until I asked if they'd ever seen a Gurkha.

'Hey, Neil, this is a good one,' exclaimed Dhal, while Dil cooed over landscapes of team pictures. No one said anything when inspecting a photo that featured only them, but quietly examined them in silent pleasure as if it would be bad form to exhibit any hubristic pride.

As family men they had taken a charming interest in my own family albums, taping and stroking the images as if they might be encouraged to come to life.

'New York, Rome, Berlin,' said Dhal in wonderment, forgetting he'd served in the States, Brunei, Kenya, Belize and even Australia and Sweden (at a piping convention where his Nepali passport caused great concern to the immigration authorities).

'This is your house, Neil?' asked Dil, 'You are a rich man!'

'No, not rich but lucky. Very lucky,' I said, a reply that brought much head nodding.

Dhal, Dil, Surendra and I later found ourselves back at Tesco, wandering down the aisles with a Nepali dictionary, buying fennel, potatoes, curry powder, diced pork and *khursarni* for our supper. Wherever Gurkhas are gathered, one night a week is set aside for the men to cook and enjoy a Nepalese feast. The boys were going to put on a gargantuan feed for Campbell, Ewen and me as a 'thank you' for the whole week. They, of course, were generously going to join us.

The little kitchen steamed up in a matter of minutes as four Gurkhas manfully toiled to prepare the vegetables and flash fry countless ingredients without burning them or each other. A vision-threatening haze stung throats and brought tears to the fearless chefs while the other brave warriors set up the table.

'You okay in there?' I asked, genuinely concerned, noting they'd all signed their names on the steamed-up window. From the depths underneath my sink, they'd salvaged a massive wok which I think last saw service on a car oil change. I'd asked Surendra to organise the water. Each place-setting now had a tea cup and saucer while the teapot was full of Highland Spring. Organised, or what?

There weren't quite enough chairs, so Chandra sat on a linen basket, but we were together in a way that few will ever know. A violinist once told me that you experience a true sense of teamship very rarely in sport, but you feel it almost every time you play in an orchestra. This was our octet, a group assembled from distant parts of the world, that had met a challenge head on, triumphed and underscored a two-hundred year old British-Gurkha harmony. You can, believe me, feel both big and small at the same time. These were the men from the roof of the world who had once been strangers but were now brothers, and Ewen, Campbell and I were now part of the fraternity. The friendship of the indomitable Gurkha fighting man was ours.

'This is chutney,' poked Dil with his knife at the tomato, onion, garlic and chilli sauce which was eaten with small baked potatoes. Branstons eat your heart out.

'What do you think makes a good Gurkha officer?' I asked.

Gyan opined: 'Well, first of all he must sweat alongside us, an officer who stays in the background is not a good one.'

'Fair enough,' said Campbell. 'And how important is it that they speak good Nepali?'

'I know one officer who keeps telling me that I should speak only English,' said Dhal. 'But he'd done a Nepali course! He gets extra pay for it all his life! But he can't speak much Nepali!'

'Okay,' I mediated: 'Anything else?' There was a long pause.

'He must love us!' blurted Chandra, to a round of laughter. I knew what he meant. Nearly all British officers do. Once you've commanded Gurhas and know you never will again, a big part of your life is over. You must respect Nepalese soldiers or the whole deal is off. 'Love' might seem too strong a word in a cynical modern world but it's applied to chocolate and football too. Perhaps Chandra was right. I've never met a former

British Gurkha officer who didn't enjoy re-living the days when he wore the crossed kurkris. Yes, you must love Gurkhas.

I had had time to put all the guys' shirts in the washing machine, along with complicated instructions as to maintaining their ownership. Using scissors, mine were left without a label, Gyan's had the right corner removed and Dhal's the left. Dil's had the left side snipped off, while Surendra's the right. Chandra's were untouched. This way we could pick them out of the laundry and know whose were whose. A simple thing but it had worked – I thought.

'I've only got three shirts,' complained Chandra. It was touching that so much value was invested in our tired red polo shirts, but the crossed kukri meant something to all of us, and Chandra especially. When the missing fourth one was discovered and Chandra's sunrise smile lit up the room, it was nearly a case of the biblical shepherd searching out the missing lamb and there being 'more rejoicing in heaven and earth'.

Although a perfect summer's evening, the south stand of the Edinburgh Military Tattoo blew cool and we were glad of our sweatshirts. Campbell had driven us to the New Town and we'd galloped up to our seats in minutes, perched before the Castle's rising basalt like kids at the panto. The musical glories of Scotland set amid a swirl of tartan was a heart-lifting feast. And capped the week: at last we could sit back and enjoy another event that encapsulated the Gurkha-Scot relationship.

'Do you know most of these guys?' I asked Dhal, pointing to the twenty or so Gurkha musicians in the massed bands.

'Know them? I know them all!'

Two days later the Gurkha drum major stopped me (in a Queen's Gurkha Signals' tie) in Princes Street and was delighted to hear that Dhal was now a sergeant. There was, however, a sense of puzzled disappointment that despite the assembled flags of the world there was no Nepalese one. I wondered why this oversight had been allowed to occur (every year, as far as I can tell) especially as the Gurkhas are an annual and celebrated feature of the whole show.

Strangely, it was the King of Norway's Royal Guard that drew the greatest applause from our guys. Not only did they perform a set of impeccable silent drill but they had a band that played a pulse-quickening tune that raised the moment even higher. When they marched off the squad broke into *Scots Wha' Hae* and the sky was broken with ecstatic applause. They can sing *too*!

Like most soldiers, though, we loved the *Black Bear*, a tune traditionally played upon exit of any retreat. 'Is very difficult,' confided Dhal. The fireworks blew and blasted into the black sky like fiery flowers. Happy, colourful explosions to cap our entire trip, it was entirely fitting and thrilling.

I had passed a note to the commentator, Alasdair Hutton, who pre-event had announced that we, the Gurkha Highlanders, were in the audience, had just walked from Mallaig to Stonehaven and had raised £55,000. The applause was stupendous and rang round the amphitheatre with loud affection. Gyan looked off balance, as if he couldn't believe what he was hearing, while the others ostentatiously clapped each other on the back as if to announce, but not too obviously, that *we* were the Gurkha Highlanders.

They all keep in touch. Dhal once phoned from Nepal on Christmas morning.

'Happy Christmas, Neil Saheb, is Dhal!'

'Jees-sus Che-rist, Dhal!'

'Oh, you got hang over?'

'No, it's only 7.15 in the morning here, that's all.'

'Ah, I read that everyone get up early on Christmas morning?'

'That's if you're aged about six!'

'Oh, well, it's after lunch here,' he added helpfully. Nepal is five hours and forty-five minutes ahead of GMT, and fifteen minutes ahead of Indian time – as a show of independence. That same holiday Gurkhas sent me packets of tea, posters and lampshades (only a Gurkha would post lampshades). Also, a beautifully embroidered tee shirt of the Pokhora range. Who else in the world embroiders tee shirts? Still, there are few in receipt of Gurkha Christmas gifts, but I'm one, and pride is too small a word.

Surendra wrote: *Nowadays were are quite busy for the Bosnia OP, so most of the days we spend in jungle anyway we doing our job well and Cpl Dil as well. I still remember the journey which was 200 miles and very difficult but at the end of the day we did it with your every little help. We think you are doing well. £50,000 is not few money, Now I realise I did something for GWT on my life and still want to do that. At last, thank your big help. God bless you long life and happiness. Sincerely Me. Surendra.*

Chandra added: *I am Chandra pr Limbu. About my knee, now it's fit and in good condition. How about you? We hope you are in good condition. How about Campbell and your brother. Give them our namastes if you meet them. Sorry for bad handrungfing. Sincerely me, Chandra*

So his full name was Chandra prasad! Gift or Blessing of the Moon. And isn't 'sincerely me' a more logical sentiment?

The next morning they were gone by 8 a.m. I put on the kettle and somehow it didn't switch itself off. The kitchen was full of steam within a minute. There on the window were the names DIL, SURENDRA, and CHANDRA. I was in no hurry to clean that pane, and wipe them away.

Returning to an empty flat that evening, I looked up at the night sky and saw a bright little scratch of light in the heavens. A shooting star. Of course, something else in nature that moves without a soundtrack. Then gone but not forgotten.

Biographical Note

Neil Griffiths is a former soldier and Fleet Street journalist. He has written for *The Guardian, The Scotsman, The Glasgow Herald, The Sunday Post, The Glasgow Evening Times, The Sun, The Edinburgh Evening News* and many magazines. Griffiths is perhaps best known as the press officer for the Scottish Poppy Appeal, The Royal British Legion and the Gurkha Welfare Trust. He is editor of the Royal British Legion Scotland's journal, *The Scottish Legion News.*

What it is all about: Limbu widow from East Nepal

Also by Neil Griffiths

Gurkha Reiver
Walking the Southern Upland Way

'The funniest book I've read about the modern Gurkha.'
Joanna Lumley

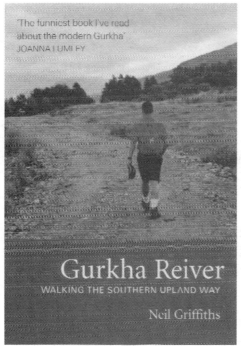

Gurkha Reiver Press Comment

Griffiths' fondness for Gurkhas radiates every page ... Buy this book.' ***Dumfries & Galloway Standard***
'Engaging ... normally I do not approve of treks, mountaineering and so on, but I am willing to bend my stern code on this occasion.' ***The Scotsman*, Rab McNeil**
'Fascinating insight into the lives and culture of the people of Nepal.' ***Sunday Post*, Rob Scott**
'A nice (Christmas) stocking filler and name checks a rogue's gallery.' ***The Scotsman*, Simon Pia**
'Written with style and humour ... buy it.' ***Soldier Magazine***
'His story fairly gallops along, rather like his four colleagues and Griffiths himself.' ***The Scotsman*, Fordyce Maxwell**
'Bound to inspire walkers ... seamlessly stitches history with travelogue ... wryly amusing.' ***Focus***
'Amusing it certainly is ... imposes on the reader what it means to be a Gurkha'. ***Border Telegraph*, Atholl Innes**

ISBN 0 9544416 0 5
Price £10.99

(Royalties go to the Gurkha Welfare Trust)

Published by Cualann Press Ltd., 6 Corpach Drive, Dunfermline, Fife KY12 7XG
Tel/Fax 01383 733724
Email cualann@btinternet.com Website www.cualann-scottish-books.co.uk